Miriam

MODERN AND CONTEMPORARY AFRO-AMERICAN POETRY

edited by

Bernard W. Bell

University of Massachusetts

Allyn and Bacon, Inc., Boston

 Library of Congress Catalog Card Number: 73-164780.

The editor is grateful to the following poets, their representatives, and publishers for permission to reprint copyrighted material:

ARNA BONTEMPS: "A Black Man Talks of Reaping," "Nocturne at Bethesda," "The Day-Breakers," "Southern Mansion," "My Heart Has Known Its Winter," and "A Note of Humility" from *Personals* by Arna Bontemps, copyright 1963 by Arna Bontemps. Reprinted by permission of Harold Ober Associates, Inc.

GWENDOLYN BROOKS: "the mother" and "the preacher: ruminates behind the sermon," copyright 1945 by Gwendolyn Brooks Blakely; "the children of the poor," copyright 1949 by Gwendolyn Brooks Blakely; "The Bean Eaters" and "We Real Cool," copyright 1959 by Gwendolyn Brooks; "The Chicago Defender Sends a Man to Little Rock" and "The Lovers of the Poor," copyright 1960 by Gwendolyn Brooks; all from *Selected Poems* by Gwendolyn Brooks. Reprinted by permission of Harper & Row, Publishers, Inc.

STERLING A. BROWN: "Southern Road," "Remembering Nat Turner," "After Winter," "The Ballad of Joe Meek," and "Strong Men" reprinted by permission of the author.

LUCILLE CLIFTON: "the lost baby poem" from manuscript; reprinted by permission of the author; "after kent state" from *The Massachusetts Review;* reprinted by permission of the author; "In the Inner City," "My Mama Moved Among the Days," "Miss Rosie," "Good Times" and "Ca'line's Prayer" from *Good Times* by Lucille Clifton, copyright 1969 by Lucille Clifton. Reprinted by permission of Random House, Inc.

COUNTEE CULLEN: "Heritage," "Yet Do I Marvel," "Simon the Cyrenian Speaks," and "Incident," copyright 1925 by Harper & Row, Publishers, Inc.; renewed 1953 by Ida M. Cullen; "Scottsboro, Too, Is Worth Its Song," copyright 1935 by Harper & Row, Publishers, Inc.; renewed 1963 by Ida M. Cullen; "From the Dark Tower," copyright 1927 by Harper & Row, Publishers, Inc.; renewed 1955 by Ida M. Cullen; all from *On These I Stand* by Countee Cullen. Reprinted by permission of Harper & Row, Publishers, Inc.

MARGARET DANNER: "I'll Walk the Tightrope," "The Elevator Man Adheres to Form," and "Far from Africa: Four Poems" reprinted by permission of the author.

FRANK MARSHALL DAVIS: "Four Glimpses of Night," "Flowers of Darkness," "Robert Whitmore," "Arthur Ridgewood, M.D.," and "Giles Johnson, Ph.D." reprinted by permission of the author.

JULIA FIELDS: "Poem," "High on the Hog," "I Heard a Young Man Saying," "Madness One Monday Evening" and "No Time for Poetry" reprinted by permission of the author.

NIKKI GIOVANNI: "Nikki-Rosa," "Adulthood," "Balances," and "For Theresa" from *Black Judgment* by Nikki Giovanni, copyright 1968 by Nikki Giovanni. Reprinted by permission of the author.

ROBERT HAYDEN: "The Diver," "Market," "Tour 5," "Homage to the Empress of the Blues," "Middle Passage," "Runagate Runagate," and "Frederick Douglass" from *Selected Poems* by Robert Hayden, copyright 1966 by Robert Hayden. Reprinted by permission of October House, Inc.

LANGSTON HUGHES: "The Negro Speaks of Rivers," "Cross," "I, Too" "The Weary Blues," "Mother to Son," and "Harlem" from *Selected Poems* by Langston Hughes, copyright 1926 by Alfred A. Knopf, Inc. and renewed 1954 by Langston Hughes; reprinted by permission of publisher; "Po' Boy Blues" from *The Dream Keeper* by Langston Hughes, copyright 1927 by Alfred A. Knopf, Inc. and renewed 1954 by Langston Hughes. Reprinted by permission of the publishers.

TED JOANS: "The Truth," "For Me Again," "Why Try," "The .38," and "O Great Black Masque" from *Black Pow-Wow* by Ted Joans, copyright 1969 by Ted Joans; reprinted by permission of Hill and Wang, Inc. and Calder and Boyars; "Lester Young," copyright 1961 by Ted Joans; reprinted by permission of the author's representative, Gunther Stuhlmann.

LeROI JONES: "The Politics of Rich Painters" from *The Dead Lecturer* by LeRoi Jones, copyright 1964 by LeRoi Jones; reprinted by permission of The Sterling Lord Agency; "Look for You Yesterday, Here You Come Today" copyright 1961 by LeRoi Jones; reprinted from *Preface To A Twenty Volume Suicide Note*, Totem/Corinth Books, New York, N. Y., 1961, with permission of the author and Ronald Hobbs Literary Agency; "Black Art," "A Poem for Black Hearts," "Poem for HalfWhite College Students" copyright 1969 by LeRoi Jones; reprinted from *Black Magic Poetry 1961-67*, Bobbs-Merrill Co., Indianapolis, Ind., 1969, with permission of Bobbs-Merrill Co. and Ronald Hobbs Literary Agency.

BOB KAUFMAN: "Benediction," "Mingus," "Walking Parker Home," "African Dream," "I Have Folded My Sorrows," "Blues Note," and "High on Life" from *Solitudes Crowded with Loneliness* by Bob Kaufman, copyright 1961, 1965 by Bob Kaufman. Reprinted by permission of New Directions Publishing Corporation.

KEORAPETSE KGOSITSILE: "Brother Malcolm's Echo," "Mandela's Sermon" and "Song for Aimé Césaire" from *Spirits Unchained* by Keorapetse Kgositsile, copyright 1969 by Keorapetse Kgositsile; reprinted by permission of Broadside Press; "The Elegance of Memory" from *For Melba* by Keorapetse Kgositsile, copyright 1970 by Keorapetse Kgositsile; reprinted by permission of Third World Press.

ETHERIDGE KNIGHT: "The Idea of Ancestry," "He Sees Through Stone," "A Love Poem," and "Apology for Apostasy" from *Poems from Prison* by Etheridge Knight, copyright 1968 by Etheridge Knight; reprinted by permission of Broadside Press; "For Black Poets Who Think of Suicide" from broadside by Etheridge Knight, copyright 1969 by Broadside Press; reprinted by permission of Broadside Press; "As You Leave Me" from *Black Poetry* ed. by Dudley Randall, copyright 1969 by Broadside Press; reprinted by permission of Broadside Press.

DON L. LEE: "the negro (a pure product of americanism)" from *Black Pride* by Don L. Lee, copyright 1968 by Don L. Lee; reprinted by permission of Broadside Press; statement on poetics, "But He Was Cool," and "a poem to complement other poems" from *Don't Cry, Scream* by Don L. Lee, copyright 1969 by Don L. Lee; reprinted by permission of Broadside Press; "Blackman/an unfinished history," "Change is Not Always Progress," "We Walk the Way of the New World," and "Move Un-noticed to be Noticed: A Nationhood Poem" from *We Walk the Way of the New World* by Don L. Lee, copyright 1970 by Don L. Lee; reprinted by permission of Broadside Press.

AUDRE LORDE: "Father Son and Holy Ghost," "A Summer Oracle," "Naturally," and "Coal" reprinted by permission of the author.

CLAUDE McKAY: "Heritage," "America," "The White House," "St. Isaac's Church, Petrograd," "Outcast," "The Lynching," and "If We Must Die" from *Selected Poems of Claude McKay*, copyright 1953 by Bookman Associates, Inc. Reprinted by permission of Twayne Publishers, Inc.

NAOMI LONG MADGETT: "Native," "The Race Question," "Mortality," and "Midway" reprinted by permission of the author.

CLARENCE MAJOR: "Longlegs," "Dismal Moment, Passing," "Flesh Line, the Space," and "Celebrated Return" by Clarence Major, copyright 1969 by Clarence

Major; reprinted by permission of the author; statement on poetics from Introduction of *New Black Poetry*, ed. by Clarence Major, copyright 1969 by International Publishers Co., Inc.; reprinted by permission of the publishers.

GLORIA C. ODEN: "Review from Staten Island," "The Carousel," "'. . . As When Emotion Too Far Exceeds its Cause,'" and "The Map" reprinted by permission of the author.

DUDLEY RANDALL: "Booker T. and W. E. B.," "The Southern Road," "Legacy: My South," and "Ballad of Birmingham" from *Poem Counterpoem* by Dudley Randall and Margaret Danner, copyright 1969 by Dudley Randall and Margaret Danner. Reprinted by permission of Broadside Press.

CONRAD KENT RIVERS: "To Richard Wright," "The Invisible Man," "The Subway," "Prelude," and "The Still Voice of Harlem" from *The Still Voice of Harlem* by Conrad Kent Rivers (London, Paul Breman, 1968); reprinted by permission of Paul Breman Limited; statement on poetics from *Sixes and Sevens* ed. by Paul Breman; reprinted by permission of Paul Breman Limited.

SONIA SANCHEZ: "last poem i'm gonna write about us," "blk/rhetoric," "right on: wite america," and "liberation/poem" from *We A BaddDDD People* by Sonia Sanchez, copyright 1970 by Sonia Sanchez Knight; reprinted by permission of the author; "malcolm" from *Homecoming* by Sonia Sanchez, copyright 1969 by Sonia Sanchez; reprinted by permission of the author.

A. B. SPELLMAN: "friends i am like you tied," "Jelly Wrote," "John Coltrane," and "When Black People Are" reprinted by permission of the author.

MELVIN B. TOLSON: "Dark Symphony" from *Rendezvous with America* by Melvin B. Tolson, copyright 1944 by Dodd, Mead & Company, Inc.; reprinted by permission of Dodd, Mead & Company, Inc.; "Lambda" from *Harlem Gallery* copyright 1965 by Twayne Publishers, Inc.; reprinted by permission of Twayne Publishers, Inc.

JEAN TOOMER: "Conversion," "Beehive," "Georgia Dusk," and "Song of the Son" from *Cane* by Jean Toomer, copyright renewed 1951 by Jean Toomer. Reprinted by permission of Liveright Publishers.

MARGARET WALKER: "For My People," "Lineage," "Molly Means," "We Have Been Believers," and "Childhood" from *For My People* by Margaret Walker, copyright 1942 by Yale University Press. Reprinted by permission of Yale University Press.

CONTENTS

Sterling A. Brown (1901)

Langston Hughes (1902-1967)

Arna Bontemps (1902)

Countee Cullen (1903-1946)

Frank Marshall Davis (1905)

Margaret Danner (1923)

Naomi Long Madgett (1923)

Gloria C. Oden (1923)

Ted Joans (1928)

Conrad Kent Rivers (1933-1968)

Etheridge Knight (1933)

LeRoi Jones (1934)

Audre Lorde (1934)

A. B. Spellman (1935)

Bob Kaufman (c. 1935)

Sonia Sanchez (1935)

Lucille Clifton (1935)

Clarence Major (1936)

Keorapetse Kgositsile (1938)

Julia Fields (1938)

Don L. Lee (1942)

Nikki Giovanni (1943)

PREFACE

The purpose of Modern and Contemporary Afro-American Poetry *is threefold: 1) to represent in some depth the best modern and contemporary black American poets; 2) to provide a collection of poems that reveals the continuity and vitality of "black" poetry; and 3) to give the reader an insight into the complex fate of being a black American.*

The multitude of black poetry anthologies that have appeared in the past ten years are either factional or not adequately representative of each poet's work. Arna Bontemps' American Negro Poetry *(1963) and Robert Hayden's* Kaleidoscope: Poems by American Poets *(1967), for example, are useful historical surveys, but most of the poets in these anthologies are represented by only two or three poems. In addition to severely limiting the number of selections per poet, Langston Hughes'* New Negro Poets: USA *(1964), LeRoi Jones' and Larry Neal's* Black Fire *(1968)—almost half of its six hundred pages are devoted to poetry—and Clarence Major's* The New Black Poetry *(1969) are primarily concerned with the theme of black consciousness. Adam Miller's* Dices or Black Bones *(1970) lacks the scope and Alan Lomax and Raoul Abdul's* 3,000 Years of Black Poetry *(1970) the depth necessary for either the general reader or the academic to realize the complex nature of the black American's poetic tradition.*

Modern and Contemporary Afro-American Poetry *offers a sizeable body of the best poetry written by black Americans, from the New Negro of the twenties to the New Breed of the sixties. Believing that anthologies can be more than mere taste manuals, I have chosen those poets and poems whose power and wisdom have illuminated for me the diversity of human experience—by whatever idiom, form of verse, or trick of voice—and have quickened my sense of understanding of the emerging new world. The absence of some talented poets is due more to practical reasons of limited time, space, and money than to any artistic or ideological idiosyncrasies. However, the reader will find that the 29 poets and 152 poems selected do constitute a coherent, well-balanced collection.*

Modern and Contemporary Afro-American Poetry *should be as useful to instructors of contemporary American poetry and creative writing as it will be to students of black literature and to general readers. Covering poets from Claude McKay to Nikki Giovanni, the anthology is arranged chronologically by the dates of birth of the poets and, where possible, the composition dates of individual poems. This arrangement enables the reader to explore the versatility of individual poets and to discover what has been happening in black poetry since the two world wars and the "black revolution" of the 1960s. Statements on poetics, biographical notes, a selected bibliography, and list of chief little magazines and black presses are also provided in the appendix.*

By way of clarification, "Negro" in this book is a socioeconomic term designating the descendants of African slaves; "black," a more prideful assertion of ethnic identity, affirms both racial and cultural distinctiveness; and "Afro-American," the most accurate of the three terms, implicitly acknowledges the legacy of the black American's slave past and African heritage.

I am most grateful to my colleague Robert Tucker for pointing out the need for this anthology and for providing assistance in the early stages of its development. I am also heavily indebted to Dudley Randall for supplying an invaluable list of addresses of the poets as well as comments on the Introduction; to Sterling Brown, my mentor, for his long-standing support and critical reading of the manuscript; and to Carrie, my wife, for her encouragement and impeccable typing.

INTRODUCTION

Rich in variety and vitality, modern and contemporary Afro-American poetry provides something for readers of all temperaments, from the dashiki-wearing militant on the block to the white aesthetician in the groves of academe. Sadly enough, however, it was not until the 1960s that gifted poets like Langston Hughes, Gwendolyn Brooks, and LeRoi Jones became available in standard classroom texts. Despite its historical exclusion from general anthologies and critical studies of American literature, one of many irrefutable examples of institutional racism, Afro-American poetry belongs to the Western literary tradition. But because there has always been a boundary in America beyond which the black man could not go, Afro-American poets have held neither literary traditions nor white middle-class American values sacred and immutable. Instead, from the unknown black bards of old to Nikki Giovanni they have expressed the bittersweet reality of black experience by either adapting traditional forms to suit their needs or creating new aesthetic forms. With this and the current interest in the concept of a black aesthetic in mind, it is useful to view the evolution of Afro-American poetry in three phases: early, modern, and contemporary.

Historically, Afro-American poetry has its roots in the African slaves' lyrical affirmation of life. It is to the black unknown bards of the spirituals and folk songs—a unique fusion of a centuries-old African sensibility and an inchoate Puritan American culture—that America is indebted for its most priceless music, those sorrowful and joyous songs that subtly yet forcefully decried oppression and celebrated the possibilities of the human spirit. And whatever is distinctively racial in the poetry of this generation of black poets is, it seems to me, attributable to the creative forces of this heritage.

From a literary point of view, black American poetry begins in 1746 with the New England slave Lucy Terry's "Bars Flight," a verse account of an Indian raid in Deerfield, Massachusetts. More important as early black poets are Jupiter Hammon, a Long Island slave, whose "An Evening Thought: Salvation by Christ, with Penitential Cries" (1760) was the first well-known broadside by an Afro-American printed in the United States; Phillis Wheatley, a Senegalese slave in Boston, whose *Poems on Various Subjects* (1773) was the first published volume of black American poetry and whose heroic couplets are as precise if not as imaginative as those of her white contemporaries; George Moses Horton, a slave at the University of North Carolina, whose love lyrics in *The Hope of Liberty* (1829) were published in a vain effort to buy his freedom; and Frances E. W. Harper, an abolitionist lecturer, whose *Poems on Miscellaneous Subjects* appeared in 1854 and who is said to have "attained greater popularity than any poet of her race prior to Dunbar." By 1871 her first book had gone into its twentieth edition. James M. Whitfield, George B. Vashon, Alberry A. Whitman, and James M. Bell also drew on the passion of poetry in the anti-slavery struggle. And with the publication of Paul Laurence Dunbar's *Oak and Ivy* (1893) and *Majors and Minors* (1895) early black American literature began to flower.

Modern Afro-American poetry, on the other hand, came into its own during the age of the Lost Generation. In revolt against what they perceived as the acquisitiveness and hollowness of the American system, postwar writers like Ernest Hemingway, Gertrude Stein, T. S. Eliot, Ezra Pound, Sherwood Anderson, and Waldo Frank led the search for new social and cultural values. At the same time, the reaction of "the whole generation of young Negro writers . . . to Toomer's *Cane*," in the words of Arna Bontemps, "marked an awakening that soon thereafter began to be called a Negro renaissance." The Negro Renaissance, also known as the Harlem Renaissance and the New Negro movement, saw the meteoric rise of such names as Claude McKay, Jean Toomer, Countee Cullen, Langston Hughes, Bill (Bojangles) Robinson, Florence Mills, Josephine Baker, Ethel Waters, Paul Robeson, Roland Hayes, Aaron Douglass, Louis Armstrong, Bessie Smith, and Duke Ellington; it was the new awakening of Afro-American art and letters.

Generally speaking, the giants of the New Negro movement turned to Africa and Afro-American folklore for a sense of tradition. In the immediate historical and social background were the Pan-African Congresses convened by W. E. B. DuBois, the pioneering studies on Africa by Carter G. Woodson, and the Back-to-Africa movement of Marcus Garvey, a Jamaican black nationalist. But the thrust of the artists, as Robert Hayden has stated, was "more aesthetic and philosophical . . . than political." Langston Hughes, a leading voice of the period, captured the feeling of aesthetic freedom that characterized the Harlem upsurge when he proclaimed:

> We younger Negro artists who create now intend to express our individual dark-skinned selves without fear or shame. We know we are

> beautiful. And ugly too. The tom-tom cries and the tom-tom laughs. If colored people are pleased, we are glad. If they are not, their displeasure doesn't matter either. We build our temples for tomorrow, strong as we know how, and we stand on top of the mountain, free within ourselves.

Toward the achievement of this end, the contests and prizes sponsored by the *Crisis* and *Opportunity*, the literary journals of the NAACP and Urban League, were of invaluable service.

Equally important in giving impetus and direction to young Negro artists of the era was Dr. Alain Locke, a professor of philosophy at Howard University. Critics have come to view his anthology, *The New Negro* (1925), as the manifesto of the movement. Containing essays by black and white scholars as well as representative selections of creative writing by young Negroes, *The New Negro* celebrates what Professor Locke optimistically considered "the attainment of a significant and satisfying new phase of group development" by Americans of African descent. Rejoicing in the new spirit and race-consciousness of the younger Negro artists, Professor Locke writes in his introductory essay:

> Each generation . . . will have its creed, and that of the present is the belief in the efficacy of collective effort, in race co-operation. This deep feeling of race is at present the mainspring of Negro life. It seems to be the outcome of the reaction to proscription and prejudice; an attempt, fairly successful on the whole, to convert a defensive into an offensive position, a handicap into an incentive. It is radical in tone, but not in purpose and only the most stupid forms of opposition, misunderstanding or persecution could make it otherwise.

But Professor Locke was by no means a separatist. He believed that Garveyism was "a transient, if spectacular, phenomenon" and that the "Negro mind reaches out as yet to nothing but American wants, American ideas." Furthermore, he expressed the prevailing sentiment of the older generation of his day when he stated that the "racialism of the Negro is no limitation or reservation with respect to American life; it is only a constructive effort to build the obstructions in the stream of his progress into an efficient dam of social energy and power."

Harlem reigned supreme as the "Cultural Capital" during this period. From all points on the globe people flocked to the city within a city, searching for shelter or stardom or swinging times: young artists from the far corners of the nation, black laborers from the South and the West Indies, blue-collar workers and blue-bloods from

Europe, and white publishers, dilettantes, and bohemians from downtown Manhattan. Harlem was the black showcase of the nation, a "Promised Land" for some and "Playland" for others. Then there were the black masses who were barred from their own cabarets and knew only the hardships of "going to meet the man" or "slaving for Miss Ann."

The acknowledged standard bearers of the Harlem Renaissance were the poets. In the spring of 1922 Claude McKay, known in his native West Indies as the Bobbie Burns of Jamaica, published his first American book of verse, *Harlem Shadows.* Following the appearance of Toomer's poetic novel in 1923, books of poetry by Negroes began pouring from the presses. The principal publications of the twenties included Countee Cullen's *Color* (1925), *Copper Sun* (1927), *The Ballad of the Brown Girl* (1927), *Caroling Dusk* (1927), and *Black Christ and Other Poems* (1929); Locke's *The New Negro* (1925); Langston Hughes' *The Weary Blues* (1926) and *Fine Clothes to the Jew* (1927); and James Weldon Johnson's *The Book of American Negro Poetry* (1922) and *God's Trombones* (1927). The avowed intention of these major poets, like most New Negro artists, was to write honestly—to explore, not to exploit Afro-American culture. But many of their white admirers were only interested in the exotic qualities of their work. As a result, the young black poets soon found themselves impaled on the horns of a dilemma. On one side were white patrons and publishers encouraging them to highlight the primitiveness and sensuality of Harlem life, while on the other were members of the black middle-class condemning them for prostituting themselves and their people rather than using their talents to demonstrate the intellectual and social parity of the race.

Because his best poetry was published before 1925, Claude McKay thought of himself as a forerunner of the New Negro movement. But whether we consider him of the old order or the new, he remains one of America's finest sonneteers. First published in the *Liberator,* "If We Must Die," McKay's most popular sonnet, was written in the wake of the race riots of 1919 and, ironically, quoted by Winston Churchill before Congress as an expression of his country's outrage and militancy during World War II. Its relevance to what the New Breed poets are saying today is apparent. Equally apparent is McKay's mastery of the conventions of the sonnet as he shapes the initial anger of the three quatrains into the firm resolve that concludes with the following couplet:

> Like men we'll face the murderous, cowardly pack,
> Pressed to the wall, dying, but fighting back!

Another superb example of McKay's craftsmanship is "America." In contrast to the defiant tone of "If We Must Die," hatred and love—the same dynamic passions so prevalent in many contemporary poems—are the delicately balanced emotions providing the tension in this sonnet. Despite the "bread of bitterness" and "tiger's tooth" of institutionalized racism, the poet perseveres and rises above reciprocal hatred. But though he paradoxically loves its "cultured hell," his situation as a marginal man in an affluent yet morally bankrupt society compels him to embrace the role of a rebel and prophet of doom:

> I stand within her walls with not a shred
> Of terror, malice, not a word or jeer.
> Darkly I gaze into the days ahead,
> And see her might and granite wonders there,
> Beneath the touch of Time's unerring hand,
> Like priceless treasures sinking in the sand.

Unlike the biting militancy of "If We Must Die," these lines are more subtle but the victory—in terms of black nationalist ideology—is pyrrhic.

Toomer's *Cane* is an experimental novel whose unique design and movement invite comparison with the works of such contemporaries as Waldo Frank and Sherwood Anderson. The book is a series of lyrical character sketches and poems affirming the sensual as well as the spiritual forces of life. Breaking with the dialect tradition of Paul Laurence Dunbar and the early James Weldon Johnson, Toomer boldly reaches out for a new and distinctive form of expression in "Song of the Son" and "Georgia Dusk."

Overshadowing his love for Keats and his remarks about wanting to be a poet and not a "Negro poet" is the fact that most of the poems in Countee Cullen's first volume of verse are characterized by the poignant treatment of racial themes. "Heritage" and "Yet Do I Marvel," two of his best known poems, are adaptations of conventional lyric forms which probe deeply into the meaning of Africa and Christianity to 20th century Afro-Americans. Neither as original as McKay nor as experimental as Toomer, Cullen was nevertheless one of the best poets of the twenties. While still a junior in college, he was publishing poetry in major national magazines; and before his graduation from college with Phi Beta Kappa honors, he saw the appearance of his award-winning *Color*. Between 1925-1926 Cullen won first or second prize in several nation-wide poetry contests. Finally, after receiving his master's degree from Harvard in 1926, he was appointed assistant editor of *Opportunity*. His principal job was writing a column, "The Dark Tower," in which he reviewed new books and commented on the literary scene. In this capacity, Cullen soon came to know most of the young black poets of the renaissance. *Caroling Dusk* presents these new voices to the public.

Unlike Cullen, who looked to Keats and Shelley as models, James Weldon Johnson turned to Afro-American folklore. His two anthologies, *The Book of American Negro Spirituals* and *The Book of American Negro Poetry*, are landmarks in the study of Afro-American culture. After criticizing the limitations of the dialect tradition of Paul Laurence Dunbar, which Johnson himself occasionally used, the author of such black classics as "O Black and Unknown Bards" and "Lift Every Voice and Sing" remarks in the preface of *The Book of American Negro Poetry:*

> What the colored poet in the United States needs to do is something like what Synge did for the Irish; . . . He needs to find a form that is freer and larger than dialect, but which will still hold the racial flavor; a form expressing the imagery, the idioms, the peculiar turns of thought, and the distinctive humor and pathos, too, of the Negro, but which will also be capable of voicing the deepest and highest emotions and aspirations, and allow of the widest range of subjects and the widest scope of treatment.

Given these sentiments, it is not surprising that Johnson abandons his own use of dialect and draws on the stock material of black preachers for the seven soul-stirring sermons in *God's Trombones.*

Langston Hughes also draws on folk material in his poetry. Rather than sermons, however, his sources are work songs, jazz, and blues. His first book of verse focuses on the night life of the Harlem cabarets and captures the sights and sounds of the Jazz Age. "Midnight Nan at Leroy's," a "Young Singer," a "Nude Young Dancer," and a "Black Dancer in the Little Savoy" are poems revealing the most important characters in *The Weary Blues.* Reflecting the hollowness of white America and the synthetic joy of Harlemites, "The rhythm of life/Is a jazz rhythm" to which the "night dark girl of the swaying hips" dances while the "sleek black boys" watch. The only sound to break the jazz rhythm is the occasional "aching emptiness" of the blues being sung by the black piano player in the title poem:

> In a deep song voice with a melancholy tone
> I heard that Negro sing, that old piano moan—
>   "Ain't got nobody in all this world,

> Ain't got nobody but ma self.
> I's gwine to quit ma frownin'
> And put ma troubles on the shelf."
> Thump, thump, thump, went his feet on the floor.
> He played a few chords then he sang some more—
> "I got the Weary Blues
> And I can't be satisfied.
> Got the Weary Blues
> And can't be satisfied—
> I ain't happy no mo'
> And I wish that I had died."
> And far into the night he crooned that tune.
> The stars went out and so did the moon.

During the Roaring Twenties both jazz and blues had racy overtones, but, as the above lines suggest, the latter music was more sincere and melancholic in quality.

Besides introducing jazz and blues rhythms into poetry, Hughes' *The Weary Blues* and *Fine Clothes to the Jew,* his second publication, reveal the sweeping scope of his artistry. For one thing, Hughes possessed an exquisite sense of both the sardonic and the sentimental. While "Cross" gives a new twist to the then popular theme of miscegenation, "The Negro Speaks of Rivers" takes us on a nostalgic return to the black American's African roots. Of greater significance is Hughes' exploration of new poetic techniques, ranging from the free verse of "Mother to Son" to the improvisational form of "Po' Boy Blues."

A highly prolific and versatile artist, Hughes is regarded as the poet laureate of black America. He took the world for his audience but, for the most part, his subject was the black man on the street: the laborers, porters, domestics, cooks, dancers, singers, and unemployed. His music was the sound of Lenox Avenue in New York, Seventh Street in Washington, and South State Street in Chicago. And his language has been appropriately called Harlemese: vibrant, rhythmic, direct, and racy.

With the crash of the stock market and the beginning of the Depression, the Harlem phase of the renaissance began to decline. Its end, according to Hughes, came in 1931. "That spring for me (and, I guess, all of us) was the end of the Harlem Renaissance. We were no longer in vogue. . . ." Since literary periods are arbitrarily circumscribed time spans marked off by more or less discernible common traits and characteristics, it is not necessary to agree on the exact date of the untimely death of the New Negro movement. But inasmuch as Hughes' classification of the period as a "vogue" has proved to be somewhat misleading for many readers, it is necessary to touch on some of the accomplishments and failures of this period.

In retrospect, the primary accomplishment of the Harlem Renaissance was to provide a national showcase for a newly awakened sense of ethnic pride. In the absence of a formal organization or literary school, the black poets of the day found a common bond in their race consciousness and desire to become their own image-makers. A close examination of their poetry reveals (1) a nostalgic interest in Africa, (2) a rediscovery and reevaluation of black folk values, (3) the elevation of members of the black masses, especially the working class, as heroes, and (4) the introduction and validation of the blues, jazz, ballads, sermons, and black vernacular as poetic material. This was the literary legacy passed on to future generations of black poets.

As for failures, they were a direct result of the fact that more than anything else the Harlem Renaissance was susceptible to the national distortions of black character and the prevailing literary emphasis on technical experimentation. Launched on their careers by well-meaning white critics or supported, sometimes literally, by wealthy white patrons, the younger Harlem poets were not always free to develop their talents as they chose. Indeed, they were frequently seduced by solicitous white admirers into resurrecting such stereotypes as the exotic primitive, the comic "coon," and the bad "nigger." Commenting on this ironic perpetuation of racial stereotypes, Alain Locke wrote:

> The Negro himself has contributed his share to this through a sort of protective social mimicry . . . forced upon him through the adverse circumstances of dependence. Through having had to appeal from the unjust stereotypes of his oppressors and traducers to those of his liberators, friends and benefactors he has had to subscribe to traditional positions from which his case has been viewed. . . .

The fact remains though that in spite of the atavism of Vachel Lindsay's "Congo," Carl Van Vechten's *Nigger Heaven,* Eugene O'Neill's *Emperor Jones,* and Du Bose Heyward's *Porgy,* they provided, as Saunders Redding has noted in another context, "further artistic sanction to the use of Negro material for other than purposes of burlesque." It was left to the contemporary generation of black poets to rebel against the patronizing attitudes of a white audience and embrace a more revolutionary poetic credo.

The breadlines and benign neglect of the New Deal and the Works Progress Administration of the thirties inspired verse of social criticism like Frank M. Davis' *Black Man's Verse* (1935) and

I Am the American Negro (1937). But the most significant publication of the decade was Sterling Brown's *Southern Road* (1932). To a period of social chaos and protest, *Southern Road* was not merely a mirroring of times that were out of joint but a sensitive and imaginative tapping of the roots of the black experience. Brown, an outstanding younger member of the Harlem Renaissance, "dug his raw material from the great mine" of the folk epics and ballads like "John Henry" and "Stagolee." As James Weldon Johnson rightly perceived nearly forty years ago, Brown "has not made mere transcriptions of this folk poetry . . . he has deepened its meanings and multiplied its implications . . . . He has, in fact, done the only thing that justifies the individual artist in taking material of this sort: he has worked it into original and genuine poetry." From the terse, rhythmic lines of "Southern Road" to the looser yet skillfully controlled free verse of such later poems as "Remembering Nat Turner" the reader is aware that a master singer of tales is at work.

In contrast to the rebellious spirit of the poetry of the twenties and thirties, the verse of the forties seems sedate. This is not to say that racial themes, social protest, and experiments in prosody are absent from Robert Hayden's *Heart-Shape in the Dust* (1940), Margaret Walker's *For My People* (1942), Melvin Tolson's *Rendezvous with America* (1944), Gwendolyn Brooks' *A Street in Bronzeville* (1945), and Owen Dodson's *Powerful Long Ladder* (1946). On the contrary, the impassioned lines of Miss Walker's "For My People" and the majestic movement of Tolson's "Dark Symphony" are classic models of the modern black poet's vision of America. At the same time, understandably, the World War II generation of black poets was primarily preoccupied with mastering all that the Anglo-American tradition could offer.

Products of an era of American criticism that repudiated didacticism in literature and advocated the concept of art for art's sake, the black poets of the forties labored diligently to perfect their craftsmanship. Whether formally trained in versification or self-taught, they experimented with both traditional and new poetic forms. Occasionally, erudition and technical virtuosity became an end in themselves. In such modes, however, a poet like Hayden was capable of producing "Runagate Runagate" and "The Diver," each being an equally valid if not equally vital expression of his dual Afro-American heritage. It is an inescapable fact that most of Hayden's best poetry, like that of every major black poet of the past fifty years, is "motivated by race."

In 1950 Gwendolyn Brooks was awarded the Pulitzer Prize for *Annie Allen* (1949). Then, as now, Miss Brooks' race consciousness was low-keyed, yet keenly felt in every line. And her lyrics pulsate with the joys and sorrows of life. Stylistically, *Annie Allen* is a masterpiece. Tracing the path of a black child's movement from innocence to experience, Miss Brooks skillfully employs adaptations of many of the major metrical patterns and stanzaic forms in the English tradition, from couplets and blank verse to sonnet sequences and free verse. In this and subsequent volumes, she maintains a remarkable balance between being a poet's poet and a poet of the people.

The younger poets of the fifties were nomadic bards whose audiences were the frequenters of Greenwich Village coffee houses and San Francisco bistros. LeRoi Jones (Amiri Baraka), Bob Kaufman, and Ted Joans were of this generation. Their chief themes were alienation, jazz, war, and death; their language was iconoclastic; and their style surrealistic and arty. Too avant-garde for the traditional literary establishment, they gave public readings and appeared in underground magazines like *Beatitude, Big Table,* and *Evergreen Review.*

As one looks back on early and modern Afro-American poetry, it should be remembered—to paraphrase Frantz Fanon, the Martiniquian psychiatrist-author who has become one of the leading theoreticians of revolution in the Third World—that the preceding generations have both resisted the tyranny of racism and helped to advance the stuggle for liberation. "We must rid ourselves," says Fanon, "of the habit now that we are in the thick of the fight, of minimizing the action of our fathers or of feigning incomprehension when considering their silence and passivity. They fought as well as they could, with the arms that they possessed then; and if the echoes of their stuggle have not resounded in the international arena, we must realize that the reason for this silence lies less in their lack of heroism than in the fundamentally different international situation of our time."

Rising like a phoenix out of the ashes of Watts, Newark, and Atlanta have come the New Breed poets of the sixties. With LeRoi Jones, the multi-talented writer, as their mentor, this generation of poets—most of them under thirty-five—has set out to create a new aesthetic and a new nation. Their credo is art for people's sake and their goal is black solidarity. Because of their scathing indictment of anything considered detrimental to the advancement of black people, some critics believe that the generating spirit of the New Breed poets is hatred. But those critics with less alien sensibilities and some background in Afro-American literature view these elements as valid though increasingly ineffective poetic conventions, and find that on a deeper level the new black poetry is rooted in a love of people and life. "You see," says Don Lee, one of the most popular new poets, "black poetry will not, necessarily, teach the people how to die, but will teach the people how to live. We must live, we must show those who control the world how to live. Redefine man and put man in his proper perspective in relation to other men and to the world."

Put another way, the New Breed poets are bearers of the legacy of the Harlem Renaissance and, at the same time, rebels without a past. A quick glance at Don Lee's "Change is Not Always Progress," Sonia Sanchez' "liberation/poem," and LeRoi Jones' "Look for You Yesterday, Here You Come Today" reveals the updated interest in Africa, the blues, and the urban black idiom. But a closer examination of these and other poems in this book, especially Jones' "Black Art," gives evidence of an unprecedented revolutionary fervor and commitment to the concept of art as weapon. In fact, much of the power of contemporary Afro-American poetry is generated by a rejection of white middle-class values and academic poetic standards. Looking neither to white critics nor posterity for fame, the poets of the sixties raise their voices in song for the black masses. Some of these songs, springing as they do from humanitarian impulses and a deep sense of race pride, are hymns to the beauty of blackness. Others are frontal attacks on the myth that white is right and on the primacy of Western values. And still others explore the everyday pleasures and pains of the black experience. The poetic sensibility we discover in the lyrics of Lucille Clifton, Conrad Kent Rivers, and Etheridge Knight, for instance, is far from mere racial chauvinism.

But given the history of Western racism and the social crisis in America, it is not surprising that the moral, political, and creative impulse of most black poets of the sixties is revolutionary. The movement is toward Islam rather than Christianity, Pan-Africanism rather than Americanism, and a black rather than white aesthetic. Published by small black presses and in underground magazines, these writers are supported by the grass roots elements of black urban communities. Two groups that immediately come to mind are LeRoi Jones' Spirit House troupe on the East Coast and Hoyt Fuller's Organization of Black American Culture (OBAC) in the Midwest. This does not mean that all New Breed poets either belong to one of these organizations or march in lock step to the same revolutionary tune. Read aloud the poems of Audre Lorde, Nikki Giovanni, and Sonia Sanchez and you will perceive distinct individualities and levels of black consciousness. They are all committed to the struggle for black liberation, yet differences in emphasis and approach give diversity to their poems. From the sensitive touch of Audre Lorde to the hard-hitting street idiom of Sonia Sanchez, we see the handwriting on the wall and hear the trumpeting voices of young prophets of a new world order.

And whether they turn to Western or African and Afro-American sources, these mythmakers and visionaries should be heard. Indeed, insofar as it is a truism that poetry must be read aloud if one really wants to tune in to the poet's vibrations, then this generation of poets must be heard if not seen reading their own poems. For only in this way can one fully appreciate the electrifying sounds and gestures that give dramatic intensity to their poetry. It is interesting to note in this regard that the techniques which some critics decry as gimmickry—unconventional capitalization, line and word spacing, abbreviations, unclosed parentheses and quotation marks, esoteric images and the like—are, in effect, derivative of T. S. Eliot, Ezra Pound, E. E. Cummings, William Carlos Williams, and Charles Olson à la LeRoi Jones.

Finally, a word of caution to the uninitiated reader. Many readers have an unconscious habit, to paraphrase Ralph Ellison, of pulling their whiteness or blackness around them too tightly when turning to black literature. So whether you agree with poets like Countee Cullen, Robert Hayden, and others included here who prefer being judged by traditional literary standards or whether you are in sympathy with LeRoi Jones, Don Lee, and the OBAC poets when they insist that black literature be judged on its own terms, beware of narrow-mindedness. For the power and wisdom of the poetry are at least as important as the color, culture, and race consciousness of the poet. Moreover, when measured by the yardstick of how it has helped to revitalize the language and to make people more acutely aware of their humanity, modern and contemporary Afro-American poetry provides ample rewards for both the scholar and general reader.

CLAUDE McKAY

If We Must Die

If we must die, let it not be like hogs
Hunted and penned in an inglorious spot,
While round us bark the mad and hungry dogs,
Making their mock at our accursed lot.
If we must die, O let us nobly die,
So that our precious blood may not be shed
In vain; then even the monsters we defy
Shall be constrained to honor us though dead!
O kinsmen! we must meet the common foe!
Though far outnumbered let us show us brave,
And for their thousand blows deal one deathblow!
What though before us lies the open grave?
Like men we'll face the murderous, cowardly pack,
Pressed to the wall, dying, but fighting back!

1919

The Lynching

His Spirit in smoke ascended to high heaven.
His father, by the cruelest way of pain,
Had bidden him to his bosom once again;
The awful sin remained still unforgiven.
All night a bright and solitary star
(Perchance the one that ever guided him,
Yet gave him up at last to Fate's wild whim)
Hung pitifully o'er the swinging char.
Day dawned, and soon the mixed crowds came to view
The ghastly body swaying in the sun.
The women thronged to look, but never a one
Showed sorrow in her eyes of steely blue.

And little lads, lynchers that were to be,
Danced round the dreadful thing in fiendish glee.

Outcast

For the dim regions whence my fathers came
My spirit, bondaged by the body, longs.
Words felt, but never heard, my lips would frame;
My soul would sing forgotten jungle songs.
I would go back to darkness and to peace,
But the great western world holds me in fee,
And I may never hope for full release
While to its alien gods I bend my knee.
Something in me is lost, forever lost,
Some vital thing has gone out of my heart,
And I must walk the way of life a ghost
Among the sons of earth, a thing apart.

For I was born, far from my native clime,
Under the white man's menace, out of time.

Heritage

Now the dead past seems vividly alive,
  And in this shining moment I can trace,
Down through the vista of the vanished years,
  Your faun-like form, your fond elusive face.

And suddenly some secret spring's released,
  And unawares a riddle is revealed,
And I can read like large, black-lettered print,
  What seemed before a thing forever sealed.

I know the magic word, the graceful thought,
  The song that fills me in my lucid hours,
The spirit's wine that thrills my body through,
  And makes me music-drunk, are yours, all yours.

I cannot praise, for you have passed from praise,
  I have no tinted thought to paint you true;
But I can feel and I can write the word:
  The best of me is but the least of you.

America

Although she feeds me bread of bitterness,
And sinks into my throat her tiger's tooth,
Stealing my breath of life, I will confess
I love this cultured hell that tests my youth!
Her vigor flows like tides into my blood,
Giving me strength erect against her hate.
Her bigness sweeps my being like a flood.
Yet as a rebel fronts a king in state,
I stand within her walls with not a shred
Of terror, malice, not a word or jeer.
Darkly I gaze into the days ahead,
And see her might and granite wonders there,
Beneath the touch of Time's unerring hand,
Like priceless treasures sinking in the sand.

The White House

Your door is shut against my tightened face,
And I am sharp as steel with discontent;
But I possess the courage and the grace
To bear my anger proudly and unbent.
The pavement slabs burn loose beneath my feet,
A chafing savage, down the decent street;
And passion rends my vitals as I pass,
Where boldly shines your shuttered door of glass.
Oh, I must search for wisdom every hour,
Deep in my wrathful bosom sore and raw,
And find in it the superhuman power
To hold me to the letter of your law!
Oh, I must keep my heart inviolate
Against the potent poison of your hate.

St. Isaac's Church, Petrograd

Bow down my soul in worship very low
And in the holy silences be lost.
Bow down before the marble Man of Woe,

Bow down before the singing angel host.
What jewelled glory fills my spirit's eye,
What golden grandeur moves the depths of me!
The soaring arches lift me up on high,
Taking my breath with their rare symmetry.

Bow down my soul and let the wondrous light
Of beauty bathe thee from her lofty throne,
Bow down before the wonder of man's might.
Bow down in worship, humble and alone,
Bow lowly down before the sacred sight
Of man's Divinity alive in stone.

c. 1922

JEAN TOOMER

Conversion

African Guardian of Souls,
Drunk with rum,
Feasting on a strange cassava,
Yielding to new words and a weak palabra
Of a white-faced sardonic god—
Grins, cries
Amen,
Shouts hosanna.

Beehive

Within this black hive to-night
There swarm a million bees;
Bees passing in and out the moon,
Bees escaping out the moon,
Bees returning through the moon,
Silver bees intently buzzing,
Silver honey dripping from the swarm of bees
Earth is a waxen cell of the world comb,
And I, a drone,
Lying on my back,
Lipping honey,
Getting drunk with silver honey,
Wish that I might fly out past the moon
And curl forever in some far-off farmyard flower.

Georgia Dusk

The sky, lazily disdaining to pursue
  The setting sun, too indolent to hold

A lengthened tournament for flashing gold,
Passively darkens for night's barbecue.

A feast of moon and men and barking hounds,
An orgy for some genius of the South
With blood-hot eyes and cane-lipped scented mouth,
Surprised in making folk-songs from soul sounds.

The sawmill blows its whistle, buzz-saws stop,
And silence breaks the bud of knoll and hill,
Soft settling pollen where plowed lands fulfill
Their early promise of a bumper crop.

Smoke from the pyramidal sawdust pile
Curls up, blue ghosts of trees, tarrying low
Where only chips and stumps are left to show
The solid proof of former domicile.

Meanwhile, the men, with vestiges of pomp,
Race memories of king and caravan,
High-priests, an ostrich, and a juju-man,
Go singing through the footpaths of the swamp.

Their voices rise . . the pine trees are guitars,
Strumming, pine-needles fall like sheets of rain . .
Their voices rise . . the chorus of the cane
Is caroling a vesper to the stars . .

O singers, resinous and soft your songs
Above the sacred whisper of the pines,
Give virgin lips to cornfield concubines,
Bring dreams of Christ to dusky cane-lipped throngs.

Song of the Son

Pour O pour that parting soul in song,
O pour it in the sawdust glow of night,
Into the velvet pine-smoke, air to-night,
And let the valley carry it along.
And let the valley carry it along.

O land and soil, red soil and sweet-gum tree,
So scant of grass, so profligate of pines,
Now just before an epoch's sun declines
Thy son, in time, I have returned to thee,
Thy son, I have in time returned to thee.

In time, for though the sun is setting on
A song-lit race of slaves, it has not set;
Though late, O soil, it is not too late yet
To catch thy plaintive soul, leaving, soon gone,
Leaving, to catch thy plaintive soul soon gone.

O Negro slaves, dark purple ripened plums,
Squeezed, and bursting in the pine-wood air,
Passing, before they stripped the old tree bare
One plum was saved for me, one seed becomes

An everlasting song, a singing tree,
Caroling softly souls of slavery,
What they were, and what they are to me,
Caroling softly souls of slavery.

MELVIN B. TOLSON

Dark Symphony

I
Allegro Moderato

Black Crispus Attucks taught
Us how to die
Before white Patrick Henry's bugle breath
Uttered the vertical
Transmitting cry:
"Yea, give me liberty or give me death."

Waifs of the auction block,
Men black and strong
The juggernauts of despotism withstood,
Loin-girt with faith that worms
Equate the wrong
And dust is purged to create brotherhood.

No Banquo's ghost can rise
Against us now,
Aver we hobnailed Man beneath the brute,
Squeezed down the thorns of greed
On Labor's brow,
Garroted lands and carted off the loot.

II
Lento Grave

The centuries-old pathos in our voices
Saddens the great white world,
And the wizardry of our dusky rhythms
Conjures up shadow-shapes of ante-bellum years:

Black slaves singing *One More River to Cross*
In the torture tombs of slave-ships,
Black slaves singing *Steal Away to Jesus*

In jungle swamps,
Black slaves singing *The Crucifixion*
In slave-pens at midnight,
Black slaves singing *Swing Low, Sweet Chariot*
In cabins of death,
Black slaves singing *Go Down, Moses*
In the canebrakes of the Southern Pharaohs.

III
Andante Sostenuto

They tell us to forget
The Golgotha we tread . . .
We who are scourged with hate,
A price upon our head.
They who have shackled us
Require of us a song,
They who have wasted us
Bid us condone the wrong.

They tell us to forget
Democracy is spurned.
They tell us to forget
The Bill of Rights is burned.
Three hundred years we slaved,
We slave and suffer yet:
Though flesh and bone rebel,
They tell us to forget!

Oh, how can we forget
Our human rights denied?
Oh, how can we forget
Our manhood crucified?
When Justice is profaned
And plea with curse is met,
When Freedom's gates are barred,
Oh, how can we forget?

IV
Tempo Primo

The New Negro strides upon the continent
In seven-league boots . . .
The New Negro

Who sprang from the vigor-stout loins
Of Nat Turner, gallows-martyr for Freedom,
Of Joseph Cinquez, Black Moses of the Amistad Mutiny,
Of Frederick Douglass, oracle of the Catholic Man,
Of Sojourner Truth, eye and ear of Lincoln's legions,
Of Harriet Tubman, Saint Bernard of the Underground Railroad.

The New Negro
Breaks the icons of his detractors,
Wipes out the conspiracy of silence,
Speaks to *his* America:

"My history-moulding ancestors
Planted the first crops of wheat on these shores,
Built ships to conquer the seven seas,
Erected the Cotton Empire,
Flung railroads across a hemisphere,
Disemboweled the earth's iron and coal,
Tunneled the mountains and bridged rivers,
Harvested the grain and hewed forests,
Sentineled the Thirteen Colonies,
Unfurled Old Glory at the North Pole,
Fought a hundred battles for the Republic."

The New Negro:
His giant hands fling murals upon high chambers,
His drama teaches a world to laugh and weep,
His music leads continents captive,
His voice thunders the Brotherhood of Labor,
His science creates seven wonders,
His Republic of Letters challenges the Negro-baiters.

The New Negro,
Hard-muscled, Fascist-hating, Democracy-ensouled,
Strides in seven-league boots
Along the Highway of Today
Toward the Promised Land of Tomorrow!

V
Larghetto

None in the Land can say
To us black men Today:

You send the tractors on their bloody path,
And create Okies for *The Grapes of Wrath.*
You breed the slum that breeds a *Native Son*
To damn the good earth Pilgrim Fathers won.

None in the Land can say
To us black men Today:
You dupe the poor with rags-to-riches tales,
And leave the workers empty dinner pails.
You stuff the ballot box, and honest men
Are muzzled by your demagogic din.

None in the Land can say
To us black men Today:
You smash stock markets with your coined blitzkriegs,
And make a hundred million guinea pigs.
You counterfeit our Christianity,
And bring contempt upon Democracy.

None in the Land can say
To us black men Today:
You prowl when citizens are fast asleep,
And hatch Fifth Column plots to blast the deep
Foundations of the State and leave the Land
A vast Sahara with a Fascist brand.

VI
Tempo di Marcia

Out of abysses of Illiteracy,
Through labyrinths of Lies,
Across waste lands of Disease . . .
We advance!

Out of dead-ends of Poverty,
Through wildernesses of Superstition,
Across barricades of Jim Crowism . . .
We advance!

With the Peoples of the World . . .
We advance!

Lambda

From the mouth of the Harlem Gallery
came a voice like a
ferry horn in a river of fog:

"Hey, man, when you gonna close this dump?
Fetch highbrow stuff for the middlebrows who
don't give a damn and the lowbrows who ain't hip!
Think you're a little high-yellow Jesus?"

No longer was I a boxer with a brain bruised
against its walls by Tyche's fists,
as I welcomed Hideho Heights,
the vagabond bard of Lenox Avenue,
whose satyric legends adhered like beggar's-lice.

"Sorry, Curator, I got here late:
my black ma birthed me in the Whites' bottom drawer,
and the Reds forgot to fish me out!"

His belly laughed and quaked
the Blakean tigers and lambs on the walls.
Haw-Haw's whale of a forefinger mocked
Max Donachie's revolutionary hero, Crispus Attucks,
in the Harlem Gallery and on Boston Commons.
"In the beginning was the Word,"
he challenged, "not the Brush!"
The scorn in the eyes that raked the gallery
was the scorn of an Ozymandias.

The metal smelted from the ore of ideas,
his grin revealed all the gold he had stored away.
"Just came from a jam session
at the Daddy-O Club," he said.
"I'm just one step from heaven
with the blues a-percolating in my head.
You should've heard old Satchmo blow his horn!
The Lord God A'mighty made no mistake
the day that cat was born!"

Like a bridegroom unloosing a virgin knot,
from an inner pocket he coaxed a manuscript.

"Just given Satchmo a one-way ticket
to Immortality," he said. "Pure inspiration!"
His lips folded about the neck of a whiskey bottle
whose label belied its white-heat hooch.
I heard a gurgle, a gurgle—a death rattle.
His eyes as bright as a parachute light,
he began to rhetorize in the grand style
of a Doctor Faustus in the dilapidated Harlem Opera House:

King Oliver of New Orleans
has kicked the bucket, but he left behind
old Satchmo with his red-hot horn
to syncopate the heart and mind.
The honky-tonks in Storyville
have turned to ashes, have turned to dust,
but old Satchmo is still around
like Uncle Sam's IN GOD WE TRUST.

Where, oh, where is Bessie Smith
with her heart as big as the blues of truth?
Where, oh, where is Mister Jelly Roll
with his Cadillac and diamond tooth?
Where, oh, where is Papa Handy
with his blue notes a-dragging from bar to bar?
Where, oh, where is bulletproof Leadbelly
with his tall tales and 12-string guitar?

Old Hip Cats,
when you sang and played the blues
the night Satchmo was born,
did you know hypodermic needles in Rome
couldn't hoodoo him away from his horn?
Wyatt Earp's legend, John Henry's, too,
is a dare and a bet to old Satchmo
when his groovy blues put headlines in the news
from the Gold Coast to cold Moscow.

Old Satchmo's
gravelly voice and tapping foot and crazy notes
set my soul on fire.
If I climbed
the seventy-seven steps of the Seventh
Heaven, Satchmo's high C would carry me higher!

Are you hip to this, Harlem? Are you hip?
On Judgment Day, Gabriel will say
after he blows his horn:
"I'd be the greatest trumpeter in the Universe,
if old Satchmo had never been born!"

STERLING A. BROWN

Strong Men

The strong men keep coming on—SANDBURG

They dragged you from homeland,
They chained you in coffles,
They huddled you spoon-fashion in filthy hatches,
They sold you to give a few gentlemen ease.

They broke you in like oxen,
They scourged you,
They branded you,
They made your women breeders,
They swelled your numbers with bastards . . .
They taught you the religion they disgraced.

You sang:
  Keep a-inchin' along
  Lak a po' inch worm . . .

You sang:
  Bye and bye
  I'm gonna lay down dis heaby load . . .

You sang:
  Walk togedder, chillen,
  Dontcha git weary . . .
      The strong men keep a-comin' on
      The strong men git stronger.

They point with pride to the roads you built for them,
They ride in comfort over the rails you laid for them.
They put hammers in your hands
And said—Drive so much before sundown.

You sang:
  Ain't no hammah
  In dis lan',
  Strikes lak mine, bebby,
  Strikes lak mine.

They cooped you in their kitchens,
They penned you in their factories,
They gave you the jobs that they were too good for,
They tried to guarantee happiness to themselves
By shunting dirt and misery to you.

You sang:
  Me an' muh baby gonna shine, shine
  Me an' muh baby gonna shine.
      The strong men keep a-comin' on
      The strong men git stronger . . .

They bought off some of your leaders
You stumbled, as blind men will . . .
They coaxed you, unwontedly soft-voiced . . .
You followed a way.
Then laughed as usual.

They heard the laugh and wondered;
Uncomfortable;
Unadmitting a deeper terror . . .
      The strong men keep a-comin' on
      Gittin' stronger . . .

What, from the slums
Where they have hemmed you,
What, from the tiny huts
They could not keep from you—
What reaches them
Making them ill at ease, fearful?
Today they shout prohibition at you
"Thou shalt not this"
"Thou shalt not that"
"Reserved for whites only"
You laugh.

One thing they cannot prohibit—
      The strong men . . . coming on

The strong men gittin' stronger.
Strong men . . .
STRONGER . . .

c. 1927

Southern Road

Swing dat hammer—hunh—
Steady, bo';
Swing dat hammer—hunh—
Steady, bo';
Ain't no rush, bebby,
Long ways to go.

Burner tore his—hunh—
Black heart away;
Burner tore his—hunh—
Black heart away;
Got me life, bebby,
An' a day.

Gal's on Fifth Street—hunh—
Son done gone;
Gal's on Fifth Street—hunh—
Son done gone;
Wife's in de ward, bebby,
Babe's not bo'n.

My ole man died—hunh—
Cussin' me;
My ole man died—hunh—
Cussin' me;
Ole lady rocks, bebby,
Huh misery.

Doubleshackled—hunh—
Guard behin';
Doubleshackled—hunh—
Guard behin';
Ball and chain, bebby,
On my min'.

White man tells me—hunh—
Dam yo' soul;
White man tells me—hunh—
Dam yo' soul;
Got no need, bebby,
To be tole.

Chain gang nevah—hunh—
Let me go;
Chain gang nevah—hunh—
Let me go;
Po' los' boy, bebby,
Evahmo'....

c. 1932

After Winter

He snuggles his fingers
In the blacker loam
The lean months are done with,
The fat to come.

His eyes are set
On a brushwood-fire
But his heart is soaring
Higher and higher.

Though he stands ragged
An old scarecrow,
This is the way
His swift thoughts go,

"Butter beans fo' Clara
Sugar corn fo' Grace
An' fo' de little feller
Runnin' space.

"Radishes and lettuce
Eggplants and beets
Turnips fo' de winter
An' candied sweets.

"Homespun tobacco
Apples in de bin
Fo' smokin' an' fo' cider
When de folks draps in."

He thinks with the winter
His troubles are gone;
Ten acres unplanted
To raise dreams on.

The lean months are done with,
The fat to come.
His hopes, winter wanderers,
Hasten home.

"Butterbeans fo' Clara
Sugar corn fo' Grace
An' fo' de little feller
Runnin' space . . . ."

The Ballad of Joe Meek

1
You cain't never tell
How far a frog will jump,
When you jes' see him planted
On his big broad rump.

Nor what a monkey's thinking
By the working of his jaws—
You jes' cain't figger;
And I knows, because

Had me a buddy,
Soft as pie
Joe Meek they called him
And they didn't lie.

The good book say
"Turn the other cheek,"
But that warn't no turning
To my boy Joe Meek.

He turned up all parts,
  And baigged you to spank,
Pulled down his breeches,
  And supplied the plank.

    The worm that didn't turn
      Was a rattlesnake to Joe:
    Wasn't scary—jes' meek, suh,
      Was made up so.

2

It was late in August
  What dey calls dog days,
Made even beetle hounds
  Git bulldog ways.

    Would make a pet bunny
      Chase a bad blood-hound,
    Make a new-born baby
      Slap his grandpa down.

The air it was muggy
  And heavy with heat,
The people all sizzled
  Like frying meat.

    The icehouse was heaven
      The pavements was hell
    Even Joe didn't feel
      So agreeable.

Strolling down Claiborne
  In the wrong end of town
Joe saw two policemen
  Knock a po' gal down.

    He didn't know her at all,
      Never saw her befo'
    But that didn't make no difference,
      To my ole boy Joe.

Walks up to the cops,
  And, very polite,

Ast them ef they thought
  They had done *just right.*

    One cracked him with his billy
      Above the left eye,
    One thugged him with his pistol
      And let him lie.

3
When he woke up, and knew
  What the cops had done,
Went to a hockshop
  Got hisself a gun.

    Felt mo' out of sorts
      Than ever befo',
    So he went on a rampage
      My ole boy Joe.

Shot his way to the station house,
  Rushed right in,
Wasn't nothing but space
  Where the cops had been.

    They called the reserves,
      And the national guard,
    Joe was in a cell
      Overlooking the yard.

The machine guns sputtered,
  Didn't faze Joe at all—
But evvytime *he* fired
  A cop would fall.

    The tear-gas made him laugh
      When they left it fly,
    Laughing gas made him hang
      His head an' cry.

He threw the hand grenades back
  With a outshoot drop,
An' evvytime he threw
  They was one less cop.

The Chief of Police said
"What kinda *man* is this?"
And held up his shirt
For a armistice.

"Stop gunning black boy,
And we'll let you go."
"I thank you very kindly,"
Said my ole boy Joe.

"We promise you safety
If you'll leave us be—"
Joe said: "That's agreeable
Sir, by me . . . ."

4
The sun had gone down
The air it was cool,
Joe stepped out on the pavement
A fighting fool.

Had walked from the jail
About half a square,
When a cop behind a post
Let him have it fair.

Put a bullet in his left side
And one in his thigh,
But Joe didn't lose
His shootin' eye.

Drew a cool bead
On the cop's broad head;
"I returns you yo' favor"
And the cop fell dead.

The next to last words
He was heard to speak
Was just what you would look for
From my boy Joe Meek.

Spoke real polite
To de folks standing by:

"Would you please do me one kindness,
Fo' I die?"

"Won't be here much longer
To bother you so,
Would you bring me a drink of water,
Fo' I go?"

The very last words
He was heard to say,
Showed a different Joe talking
In a different way.

"Ef my bullets weren't gone,
An' my strength all spent—
I'd send the chief something
With a compliment."

"And we'd race to hell,
And I'd best him there,
Like I would of done here
Ef he'd played me fair."

5
So you cain't never tell
How fas' a dog can run
When you see him a-sleeping,
In the sun.

Remembering Nat Turner

We saw a bloody sunset over Courtland, once Jerusalem,
As we followed the trail that old Nat took
When he came out of Cross Keys down upon Jerusalem,
In his angry stab for freedom a hundred years ago.
The land was quiet, and the mist was rising,
Out of the woods and the Nottaway swamp,
Over Southampton the still night fell,
As we rode down to Cross Keys where the march began.

When we got to Cross Keys, they could tell us little of him,
The Negroes had only the faintest recollections:
"I ain't been here so long, I come from up roun' Newsome;
Yassah, a town a few miles up de road,
The old folks who coulda told you is all dead an' gone.
I heard something, sometime; I doan jis remember what.
'Pears lak I heard that name somewheres or other.
So he fought to be free. Well. You doan say."

An old white woman recalled exactly
How Nat crept down the steps, axe in his hand,
After murdering a woman and child in bed,
"Right in this here house at the head of these stairs"
(In a house built long after Nat was dead).
She pointed to a brick store where Nat was captured,
(Nat was taken in the swamp, three miles away)
With his men around him, shooting from the windows
(She was thinking of Harper's Ferry and old John Brown).
She cackled as she told how they riddled Nat with bullets
(Nat was tried and hanged at Courtland, ten miles away).
She wanted to know why folks would comes miles
Just to ask about an old nigger fool.
"Ain't no slavery no more, things is going all right,
Pervided thar's a good goober market this year.
We had a sign post here with printing on it,
But it rotted in the hole, and thar it lays,
And the nigger tenants split the marker for kindling.
Things is all right, naow, ain't no trouble with the niggers
Why they make this big to-do over Nat?"

As we drove from Cross Keys back to Courtland,
Along the way that Nat came down upon Jerusalem,
A watery moon was high in the cloud-filled heavens,
The same moon he dreaded a hundred years ago.
The tree they hanged Nat on is long gone to ashes,
The trees he dodged behind have rotted in the swamps.

The bus for Miami and the trucks boomed by,
And touring cars, their heavy tires snarling on the pavement.
Frogs piped in the marshes, and a hound bayed long,
And yellow lights glowed from the cabin windows.

As we came back the way that Nat led his army,
Down from Cross Keys, down to Jerusalem,

We wondered if his troubled spirit still roamed the Nottaway,
Or if it fled with the cock-crow at daylight,
Or lay at peace with the bones in Jerusalem,
Its restlessness stifled by Southampton clay.
We remembered the poster rotted through and falling,
The marker split for kindling a kitchen fire.

LANGSTON HUGHES

The Negro Speaks of Rivers

I've known rivers:
I've known rivers ancient as the world and older than the flow of human blood in human veins.

My soul has grown deep like the rivers.

I bathed in the Euphrates when dawns were young.
I built my hut near the Congo and it lulled me to sleep.
I looked upon the Nile and raised the pyramids above it.
I heard the singing of the Mississippi when Abe Lincoln went down to New Orleans, and I've seen its muddy bosom turn all golden in the sunset.

I've known rivers:
Ancient, dusky rivers.

My soul has grown deep like the rivers.

1921

Mother to Son

Well, son, I'll tell you:
Life for me ain't been no crystal stair.
It's had tacks in it,
And splinters,
And boards torn up,
And places with no carpet on the floor—
Bare.
But all the time
I'se been a-climbin' on,
And reachin' landin's,
And turnin' corners,
And sometimes goin' in the dark

Where there ain't been no light.
So, boy, don't you turn back.
Don't you set down on the steps
'Cause you finds it's kinder hard.
Don't you fall now—
For I'se still goin', honey,
I'se still climbin',
And life for me ain't been no crystal stair.

1922

Cross

My old man's a white old man
And my old mother's black.
If ever I cursed my white old man
I take my curses back.

If ever I cursed my black old mother
And wished she were in hell,
I'm sorry for that evil wish
And now I wish her well.

My old man died in a fine big house.
My ma died in a shack.
I wonder where I'm gonna die,
Being neither white nor black?

1925

The Weary Blues

Droning a drowsy syncopated tune,
Rocking back and forth to a mellow croon,
        I heard a Negro play.
Down on Lenox Avenue the other night
By the pale dull pallor of an old gas light
        He did a lazy sway . . . .
        He did a lazy sway . . . .
To the tune o' those Weary Blues.
With his ebony hands on each ivory key
He made that poor piano moan with melody.
        O Blues!

Swaying to and fro on his rickety stool
He played that sad raggy tune like a musical fool
        Sweet Blues!
Coming from a black man's soul.
        O Blues!
In a deep song voice with a melancholy tone
I heard that Negro sing, that old piano moan—
        "Ain't got nobody in all this world,
        Ain't got nobody but ma self.
        I's gwine to quit ma frownin'
        And put ma troubles on the shelf."
Thump, thump, thump, went his foot on the floor.
He played a few chords then he sang some more—
        "I got the Weary Blues
        And I can't be satisfied.
        Got the Weary Blues
        And can't be satisfied—
        I ain't happy no mo'
        And I wish that I had died."
And far into the night he crooned that tune.
The stars went out and so did the moon.
The singer stopped playing and went to bed
While the Weary Blues echoed through his head.
He slept like a rock or a man that's dead.

1925

I, Too

I, too, sing America.

I am the darker brother.
They send me to eat in the kitchen
When company comes,
But I laugh,
And eat well,
And grow strong.

Tomorrow,
I'll sit at the table
When company comes.
Nobody'll dare

Say to me,
"Eat in the kitchen,"
Then.

Besides,
They'll see how beautiful I am
And be ashamed—

I, too, am America.

Po' Boy Blues

When I was home de
Sunshine seemed like gold
When I was home de
Sunshine seemed like gold.
Since I come up North de
Whole damn world's turned cold.

I was a good boy,
Never done no wrong.
Yes, I was a good boy,
Never done no wrong,
But this world is weary
An' de road is hard an' long.

I fell in love with
A gal I thought was kind.
Fell in love with
A gal I thought was kind.
She made me lose ma money
An' almost lose ma mind.

Weary, weary,
Weary, early in de morn.
Weary, weary,
Early, early in de morn.
I's so weary
I wish I'd never been born.

1926

Harlem

What happens to a dream deferred?

Does it dry up
like a raisin in the sun?
Or fester like a sore—
And then run?
Does it stink like rotten meat?
Or crust and sugar over
like a syrupy sweet?

Maybe it just sags
like a heavy load

Or does it explode?

ARNA BONTEMPS

The Day-Breakers

We are not come to wage a strife
  With swords upon this hill;
It is not wise to waste the life
  Against a stubborn will.
Yet would we die as some have done:
Beating a way for the rising sun.

1924

A Black Man Talks of Reaping

I have sown beside all waters in my day.
I planted deep, within my heart the fear
That wind or fowl would take the grain away.
I planted safe against this stark, lean year.

I scattered seed enough to plant the land
In rows from Canada to Mexico
But for my reaping only what the hand
Can hold at once is all that I can show.

Yet what I sowed and what the orchard yields
My brother's sons are gathering stalk and root,
Small wonder then my children glean in fields
They have not sown, and feed on bitter fruit.

1925

Nocturne at Bethesda

I thought I saw an angel flying low,
I thought I saw the flicker of a wing
Above the mulberry trees; but not again.

Bethesda sleeps. That ancient pool that healed
A host of bearded Jews does not awake.

This pool that once the angels troubled does not move
No angel stirs it now, no Saviour comes
With healing in His hands to raise the sick
And bid the lame man leap upon the ground.

The golden days are gone. Why do we wait
So long upon the marble steps, blood
Falling from our open wounds? and why
Do our black faces search the empty sky?
Is there something we have forgotten? some precious thing
We have lost, wandering in strange lands?

There was a day, I remember now,
I beat my breast and cried, "Wash me God,
Wash me with a wave of wind upon
The barley; O quiet One, draw near, draw near!
Walk upon the hills with lovely feet
And in the waterfall stand and speak.

"Dip white hands in the lily pool and mourn
Upon the harps still hanging in the trees
Near Babylon along the river's edge,
But oh, remember me, I pray, before
The summer goes and rose leaves lose their red."

The old terror takes my heart, the fear
Of quiet waters and of faint twilights.
There will be better days when I am gone
And healing pools where I cannot be healed.
Fragrant stars will gleam forever and ever
Above the place where I lie desolate.

Yet I hope, still I long to live.
And if there can be returning after death
I shall come back. But it will not be here;
If you want me you must search for me
Beneath the palms of Africa. Or if
I am not there then you may call to me
Across the shining dunes, perhaps I shall
Be following a desert caravan.

I may pass through centuries of death
With quiet eyes, but I'll remember still
A jungle tree with burning scarlet birds.
There is something I have forgotten, some precious thing.
I shall be seeking ornaments of ivory,
I shall be dying for a jungle fruit.

You do not hear, Bethesda.
O still green water in a stagnant pool!
Love abandoned you and me alike.
There was a day you held a rich full moon
Upon your heart and listened to the words
Of men now dead and saw the angels fly.
There is a simple story on your face;
Years have wrinkled you. I know, Bethesda!
You are sad. It is the same with me.

1926

My Heart Has Known Its Winter

A little while spring will claim its own,
in all the land around for mile on mile
tender grass will hide the rugged stone.
My still heart will sing a little while,

And men will never think this wilderness
was barren once when grass is over all,
hearing laughter they may never guess
my heart has known its winter and carried gall.

1926

Southern Mansion

Poplars are standing there still as death
And ghosts of dead men
Meet their ladies walking
Two by two beneath the shade
And standing on the marble steps.

There is a sound of music echoing
Through the open door

And in the field there is
Another sound tinkling in the cotton:
Chains of bondmen dragging on the ground.

The years go back with an iron clank,
A hand is on the gate,
A dry leaf trembles on the wall.
Ghosts are walking.
They have broken roses down
And poplars stand there still as death.

1930

A Note of Humility

When all our hopes are sown on stony ground,
And we have yielded up the thought of gain,
Long after our last songs have lost their sound,
We may come back, we may come back again.

When thorns have choked the last green thing we loved,
And we have said all that there is to say,
When love that moved us once leaves us unmoved,
Then men like us may come to have a day.

For it will be with us as with the bee,
The meager ant, the sea-gull and the loon;
We may come back to triumph mournfully
An hour or two, but it will not be soon.

1932

COUNTEE CULLEN

Heritage

(FOR HAROLD JACKMAN)

What is Africa to me:
Copper sun or scarlet sea,
Jungle star or jungle track,
Strong bronzed men, or regal black
Women from whose loins I sprang
When the birds of Eden sang?
One three centuries removed
From the scenes his fathers loved,
Spicy grove, cinnamon tree,
What is Africa to me?

So I lie, who all day long
Want no sound except the song
Sung by wild barbaric birds
Goading massive jungle herds,
Juggernauts of flesh that pass
Trampling tall defiant grass
Where young forest lovers lie,
Plighting troth beneath the sky.
So I lie, who always hear,
Though I cram against my ear
Both my thumbs, and keep them there,
Great drums throbbing through the air.
So I lie, whose fount of pride,
Dear distress, and joy allied,
Is my somber flesh and skin,
With the dark blood dammed within
Like great pulsing tides of wine
That, I fear, must burst the fine
Channels of the chafing net
Where they surge and foam and fret.

Africa? A book one thumbs
Listlessly, till slumber comes.
Unremembered are her bats
Circling through the night, her cats
Crouching in the river reeds,
Stalking gentle flesh that feeds
By the river brink; no more
Does the bugle-throated roar
Cry that monarch claws have leapt
From the scabbards where they slept.
Silver snakes that once a year
Doff the lovely coats you wear,
Seek no covert in your fear
Lest a mortal eye should see;
What's your nakedness to me?
Hear no leprous flowers rear
Fierce corollas in the air;
Here no bodies sleek and wet,
Dripping mingled rain and sweat,
Tread the savage measures of
Jungle boys and girls in love.
What is last year's snow to me,
Last year's anything? The tree
Budding yearly must forget
How its past arose or set—
Bough and blossom, flower, fruit,
Even what shy bird with mute
Wonder at her travail there,
Meekly labored in its hair.
One three centuries removed
From the scenes his fathers loved,
Spicy grove, cinnamon tree,
What is Africa to me?

So I lie, who find no peace
Night or day, no slight release
From the unremittant beat
Made by cruel padded feet
Walking through my body's street.
Up and down they go, and back,
Treading out a jungle track.
So I lie, who never quite
Safely sleep from rain at night—
I can never rest at all

When the rain begins to fall;
Like a soul gone mad with pain
I must match its weird refrain;
Ever must I twist and squirm,
Writhing like a baited worm,
While its primal measures drip
Through my body, crying, "Strip!
Doff this new exuberance.
Come and dance the Lover's Dance!"
In an old remembered way
Rain works on me night and day.

Quaint, outlandish heathen gods
Black men fashion out of rods,
Clay, and brittle bits of stone,
In a likeness like their own,
My conversion came high-priced;
I belong to Jesus Christ,
Preacher of humility
Heathen gods are naught to me.

Father, Son, and Holy Ghost,
So I make an idle boast;
Jesus of the twice-turned cheek,
Lamb of God, although I speak
With my mouth thus, in my heart
Do I play a double part.
Ever at Thy glowing altar
Must my heart grow sick and falter,
Wishing He I served were black,
Thinking then it would not lack
Precedent of pain to guide it,
Let who would or might deride it;
Surely then this flesh would know
Yours had borne a kindred woe.
Lord, I fashion dark gods, too,
Daring even to give You
Dark despairing features where
Crowned with dark rebellious hair,
Patience wavers just so much as
Mortal grief compels, while touches
Quick and hot, of anger, rise
To smitten cheek and weary eyes.
Lord, forgive me if my need

Sometimes shapes a human creed.
All day long and all night through,
One thing only must I do:
Quench my pride and cool my blood,
Lest I perish in the flood,
Lest a hidden ember set
Timber that I thought was wet
Burning like the dryest flax,
Melting like the merest wax,
Lest the grave restore its dead.
Not yet has my heart or head
In the least way realized
They and I are civilized.

Simon the Cyrenian Speaks

He never spoke a word to me,
And yet He called my name;
He never gave a sign to me,
And yet I knew and came.

At first I said, "I will not bear
His cross upon my back;
He only seeks to place it there
Because my skin is black."

But He was dying for a dream,
And He was very meek,
And in His eyes there shone a gleam
Men journey far to seek.

It was Himself my pity bought;
I did for Christ alone
What all of Rome could not have wrought
With bruise of lash or stone.

1924

Yet Do I Marvel

I doubt not God is good, well-meaning, kind,
And did He stoop to quibble could tell why

The little buried mole continues blind,
Why flesh that mirrors Him must some day die,
Make plain the reason tortured Tantalus
Is baited by the fickle fruit, declare
If merely brute caprice dooms Sisyphus
To struggle up a never-ending stair.
Inscrutable His ways are, and immune
To catechism by a mind too strewn
With petty cares to slightly understand
What awful brain compels His awful hand.
Yet do I marvel at this curious thing:
To make a poet black, and bid him sing!

Incident

Once riding in old Baltimore
Heart-filled, head-filled with glee,
I saw a Baltimorean
Keep looking straight at me.

Now I was eight and very small,
And he was no whit bigger,
And so I smiled, but he poked out
His tongue, and called me, "Nigger."

I saw the whole of Baltimore
From May until December;
Of all the things that happened there
That's all that I remember.

From the Dark Tower

We shall not always plant while others reap
The golden increment of bursting fruit,
Not always countenance, abject and mute,
That lesser men should hold their brothers cheap;
Not everlastingly while others sleep
Shall we beguile their limbs with mellow flute,
Not always bend to some more subtle brute;
We were not made eternally to weep.

The night whose sable breast relieves the stark
White stars is no less lovely being dark,
And there are buds that cannot bloom at all
In light, but crumple, piteous, and fall;
So in the dark we hide the heart that bleeds,
And wait, and tend our agonizing seeds.

1926

Scottsboro, Too, Is Worth Its Song

(A POEM TO AMERICAN POETS)

I said:

Now will the poets sing,—
Their cries go thundering
Like blood and tears
Into the nation's ears,
Like lightning dart
Into the nation's heart.
Against disease and death and all things fell,
And war,
Their strophes rise and swell
To jar
The foe smug in his citadel.

Remembering their sharp and pretty
Tunes for Saccò and Vanzetti,
I said:
Here too's a cause divinely spun
For those whose eyes are on the sun,
Here in epitome
Is all disgrace
And epic wrong,
Like wine to brace
The minstrel heart, and blare it into song.

Surely, I said,
Now will the poets sing.
  But they have raised no cry.
  I wonder why.

1932

FRANK MARSHALL DAVIS

Giles Johnson, Ph.D.

Giles Johnson
had four college degrees
knew the whyfore of this
and wherefore of that
could orate in Latin
or Cuss in Greek
and, having learned such things
he died of starvation
because he wouldn't teach
and he couldn't porter.

1931

Robert Whitmore

Having attained success in business
possessing three cars
one wife and two mistresses
a home and furniture
talked of by the town
and thrice ruler of the local Elks
Robert Whitmore
died of apoplexy
when a stranger from Georgia
mistook him
for a former Macon waiter.

1933

Arthur Ridgewood, M.D.

He debated whether
as a poet
to have dreams and beans
or as a physician

have a long car and caviar.
Dividing his time between both
he died from a nervous breakdown
caused by worry
from rejection slips
and final notices from the finance company.

1933

Four Glimpses of Night

I

Eagerly
Like a woman hurrying to her lover
Night comes to the room of the world
And lies, yielding and content
Against the cool round face
Of the moon.

II

Night is a curious child, wandering
Between earth and sky, creeping
In windows and doors, daubing
The entire neighborhood
With purple paint.
Day
Is an apologetic mother
Cloth in hand
Following after.

III

Peddling
From door to door
Night sells
Black bags of peppermint stars
Heaping cones of vanilla moon
Until
His wares are gone
Then shuffles homeward
Jingling the gray coins
of daybreak.

IV

Night's brittle song, silver-thin
Shatters into a billion fragments
Of quiet shadows
At the blaring jazz
Of a morning sun.

1935

Flowers of Darkness

Slowly the night blooms, unfurling
Flowers of darkness, covering
The trellised sky, becoming
A bouquet of blackness
Unending
Touched with sprigs
Of pale and budding stars

Soft the night smell
Among April trees
Soft and richly rare
Yet commonplace
Perfume on a cosmic scale

I turn to you Mandy Lou
I see the flowering night
Cameo condensed
Into the lone black rose
Of your face

The young woman-smell
Of your poppy body
Rises to my brain as opium
Yet silently motionless
I sit with twitching fingers
Yea, even reverently

Sit I
With you and the blossoming night
For what flower, plucked,
Lingers long?

1936

ROBERT HAYDEN

Frederick Douglass

When it is finally ours, this freedom, this liberty, this beautiful
and terrible thing, needful to man as air,
usable as earth; when it belongs at last to all,
when it is truly instinct, brain matter, diastole, systole,
reflex action; when it is finally won; when it is more
than the gaudy mumbo jumbo of politicians:
this man, this Douglass, this former slave, this Negro
beaten to his knees, exiled, visioning a world
where none is lonely, none hunted, alien,
this man, superb in love and logic, this man
shall be remembered. Oh, not with statues' rhetoric,
not with legends and poems and wreaths of bronze alone,
but with the lives grown out of his life, the lives
fleshing his dream of the beautiful, needful thing.

c. 1944

Middle Passage

I.

Jesús, Estrella, Esperanza, Mercy:
Sails flashing to the wind like weapons,
sharks following the moans the fever and the dying;
horror the corposant and compass rose.

Middle Passage:
voyage through death
to life upon these shores.

"10 April 1800—
Blacks rebellious. Crew uneasy. Our linguist says
their moaning is a prayer for death,
ours and their own. Some try to starve themselves.

Lost three this morning leaped with crazy laughter
to the waiting sharks, sang as they went under."

Desire, Adventure, Tartar, Ann:

Standing to America, bringing home
black gold, black ivory, black seed.

Deep in the festering hold thy father lies,
of his bones New England pews are made,
those are altar lights that were his eyes.

Jesus Saviour Pilot Me
Over Life's Tempestuous Sea

We pray that Thou wilt grant, O Lord
safe passage to our vessels bringing
heathen souls unto Thy chastening.

Jesus Saviour

"8 bells. I cannot sleep, for I am sick
with fear, but writing eases fear a little
since still my eyes can see these words take shape
upon the page & so I write, as one
would turn to exorcism. 4 days scudding,
but now the sea is calm again. Misfortune
follows in our wake like sharks (our grinning
tutelary gods). Which one of us
has killed an albatross? A plague among
our blacks—Ophthalmia: blindness—& we
have jettisoned the blind to no avail.
It spreads, the terrifying sickness spreads.
Its claws have scratched sight from the Capt.'s eyes
& there is blindness in the fo'c'sle
& we must sail 3 weeks before we come
to port."

What port awaits us, Davy Jones'
or home? I've heard of slavers drifting, drifting,
playthings of wind and storm and chance, their crews
gone blind, the jungle hatred
crawling up on deck.

Thou Who Walked On Galilee

"Deponent further sayeth *The Bella J*
left the Guinea Coast
with cargo of five hundred blacks and odd
for the barracoons of Florida:

"That there was hardly room 'tween-decks for half
the sweltering cattle stowed spoon-fashion there;
that some went mad of thirst and tore their flesh
and sucked the blood:

"That Crew and Captain lusted with the comeliest
of the savage girls kept naked in the cabins;
that there was one they called The Guinea Rose
and they cast lots and fought to lie with her:

"That when the Bo's'n piped all hands, the flames
spreading from starboard already were beyond
control, the negroes howling and their chains
entangled with the flames:

"That the burning blacks could not be reached,
that the Crew abandoned ship,
leaving their shrieking negresses behind,
that the Captain perished drunken with the wenches:

"Further Deponent sayeth not."

Pilot Oh Pilot Me

II.

Aye, lad, and I have seen those factories,
Gambia, Rio Pongo, Calabar;
have watched the artful mongos baiting traps
of war wherein the victor and the vanquished

Were caught as prizes for our barracoons.
Have seen the nigger kings whose vanity
and greed turned wild black hides of Fellatah,
Mandingo, Ibo, Kru to gold for us.

And there was one—King Anthracite we named him—
fetish face beneath French parasols
of brass and orange velvet, impudent mouth
whose cups were carven skulls of enemies:

He'd honor us with drum and feast and conjo
and palm-oil glistening wenches deft in love,
and for tin crowns that shone with paste,
red calico and German-silver trinkets

Would have the drums talk war and send
his warriors to burn the sleeping villages
and kill the sick and old and lead the young
in coffles to our factories.

Twenty years a trader, twenty years,
for there was wealth aplenty to be harvested
from those black fields, and I'd be trading still
but for the fevers melting down my bones.

III.

Shuttles in the rocking loom of history,
the dark ships move, the dark ships move,
their bright ironical names
like jests of kindness on a murderer's mouth;
plough through thrashing glister toward
fata morgana's lucent melting shore,
weave toward New World littorals that are
mirage and myth and actual shore.

Voyage through death,
            voyage whose chartings are unlove.

A charnel stench, effluvium of living death
spread outward from the hold,
where the living and the dead, the horribly dying,
lie interlocked, lie foul with blood and excrement.

> *Deep in the festering hold thy father lies,*
> *the corpse of mercy rots with him,*
> *rats eat love's rotten gelid eyes.*

But, oh, the living look at you
with human eyes whose suffering accuses you,
whose hatred reaches through the swill of dark
to strike you like a leper's claw.

You cannot stare that hatred down
or chain the fear that stalks the watches
and breathes on you its fetid scorching breath;
cannot kill the deep immortal human wish,
the timeless will.

"But for the storm that flung up barriers
of wind and wave, *The Amistad,* señores,
would have reached the port of Príncipe in two,
three days at most; but for the storm we should
have been prepared for what befell.
Swift as the puma's leap it came. There was
that interval of moonless calm filled only
with the water's and the rigging's usual sounds,
then sudden movement, blows and snarling cries
and they had fallen on us with machete
and marlinspike. It was as though the very
air, the night itself were striking us.
Exhausted by the rigors of the storm,
we were no match for them. Our men went down
before the murderous Africans. Our loyal
Celestino ran from below with gun
and lantern and I saw, before the cane-
knife's wounding flash, Cinquez,
that surly brute who calls himself a prince,
directing, urging on the ghastly work.
He hacked the poor mulatto down, and then
he turned on me. The decks were slippery
when daylight finally came. It sickens me
to think of what I saw, of how these apes
threw overboard the butchered bodies of
our men, true Christians all, like so much jetsam.
Enough, enough. The rest is quickly told:
Cinquez was forced to spare the two of us
you see to steer the ship to Africa,
and we like phantoms doomed to rove the sea
voyaged east by day and west by night,

deceiving them, hoping for rescue,
prisoners on our own vessel, till
at length we drifted to the shores of this
your land, America, where we were freed
from our unspeakable misery. Now we
demand, good sir, the extradition of
Cinquez and his accomplices to La
Havana. And it distresses us to know
there are so many here who seem inclined
to justify the mutiny of these blacks.
We find it paradoxical indeed
that you whose wealth, whose tree of liberty
are rooted in the labor of your slaves
should suffer the august John Quincy Adams
to speak with so much passion of the right
of chattel slaves to kill their lawful masters
and with his Roman rhetoric weave a hero's
garland for Cinquez. I tell you that
we are determined to return to Cuba
with our slaves and there see justice done. Cinquez—
or let us say 'the Prince'—Cinquez shall die."

The deep immortal human wish,
the timeless will:

Cinquez its deathless primaveral image,
life that transfigures many lives.

Voyages through death
to life upon these shores.

c. 1944

Runagate Runagate

I.

Run falls rises stumbles on from darkness into darkness
and the darkness thicketed with shapes of terror
and the hunters pursuing and the hounds pursuing
and the night cold and the night long and the river
to cross and the jack-muh-lanterns beckoning beckoning

and blackness ahead and when shall I reach that somewhere
morning and keep on going and never turn back and keep on going

Runagate
Runagate
Runagate

Many thousands rise and go
many thousands crossing over

O mythic North
O star-shaped yonder Bible city

Some go weeping and some rejoicing
some in coffins and some in carriages
some in silks and some in shackles

Rise and go or fare you well

No more auction block for me
no more driver's lash for me

If you see my Pompey, 30 yrs of age,
new breeches, plain stockings, negro shoes;
if you see my Anna, likely young mulatto
branded E on the right cheek, R on the left,
catch them if you can and notify subscriber.
Catch them if you can, but it won't be easy.
They'll dart underground when you try to catch them,
plunge into quicksand, whirlpools, mazes,
turn into scorpions when you try to catch them.

And before I'll be a slave
I'll be buried in my grave

North star and bonanza gold
I'm bound for the freedom, freedom-bound
and oh Susyanna don't you cry for me

Runagate

Runagate

II.

Rises from their anguish and their power,

Harriet Tubman,

woman of earth, whipscarred,
a summoning, a shining

Mean to be free

And this was the way of it, brethren brethren,
way we journeyed from Can't to Can.
Moon so bright and no place to hide,
the cry up and the patterollers riding,
hound dogs belling in bladed air.
And fear starts a-murbling, Never make it,
we'll never make it. *Hush that now,*
and she's turned upon us, levelled pistol
glinting in the moonlight:
Dead folks can't jaybird-talk, she says;
you keep on going now or die, she says.

Wanted   Harriet Tubman   alias The General
alias Moses   Stealer of Slaves

In league with Garrison   Alcott   Emerson
Garrett   Douglass   Thoreau   John Brown

Armed and known to be Dangerous

Wanted   Reward   Dead or Alive

Tell me, Ezekiel, oh tell me do you see
mailed Jehovah coming to deliver me?

Hoot-owl calling in the ghosted air,
five times calling to the hants in the air.
Shadow of a face in the scary leaves,
shadow of a voice in the talking leaves:

Come ride-a my train

Oh that train, ghost-story train
through swamp and savanna movering movering,
over trestles of dew, through caves of the wish,
Midnight Special on a sabre track movering movering,
first stop Mercy and the last Hallelujah.

Come ride-a my train

Mean mean mean to be free.

c. 1945

Homage to the Empress of the Blues

Because there was a man somewhere in a candystripe silk shirt,
gracile and dangerous as a jaguar and because a woman moaned
for him in sixty-watt gloom and mourned him Faithless Love
Twotiming Love Oh Love Oh Careless Aggravating Love,

She came out on the stage in yards of pearls, emerging like
a favorite scenic view, flashed her golden smile and sang.

Because grey laths began somewhere to show from underneath
torn hurdygurdy lithographs of dollfaced heaven;
and because there were those who feared alarming fists of snow
on the door and those who feared the riot-squad of statistics.

She came out on the stage in ostrich feathers, beaded satin,
and shone that smile on us and sang.

c. 1947

Tour 5

The road winds down through autumn hills
in blazonry of farewell scarlet
and recessional gold,
past cedar groves, through static villages
whose names are all that's left
of Choctaw, Chickasaw.

We stop a moment in a town
watched over by Confederate sentinels,

buy gas and ask directions of a rawboned man
whose eyes revile us as the enemy.

Shrill gorgon silence breathes behind
his taut civility
and in the ever-tautening air,
dark for us despite its Indian summer glow.
We drove on, following the route
of highwaymen and phantoms,

Of slaves and armies.
Children, wordless and remote,
wave at us from kindling porches.
And now the land is flat for miles,
the landscape lush, metallic, flayed,
its brightness harsh as bloodstained swords.

1950s

Market

Ragged boys
lift sweets, haggle
for acid-green
and bloody gelatins.
A broken smile
dandles its weedy
cigarette
over papayas too ripe
and pyramids
of rotting oranges.
Turkeys like feather-
duster flowers
lie trussed in bunchy smother.
The barefoot cripple
foraging crawls
among rinds, orts,
chewed butts, trampled
peony droppings—
his hunger litany
and suppliant before
altars of mamey,
pineapple, mango.

Turistas pass.
Por caridad, por caridad.
Lord, how they stride
on the hard good legs
money has made them.
Ay! you creatures
who have walked
on seas of money all
your foreign lives!
Por caridad.
Odor of a dripping
carcass moans
beneath the hot
fragrance of carnations,
cool scent of lilies.
Starveling dogs
hover in the reek
of frying; ashy feet
(the twistfoot beggar laughs)
kicks at them in vain.
Aloft, the Fire King's
flashing mask of tin
looks down with eyes
of sunstruck glass.

c. 1958

The Diver

Sank through easeful
azure. Flower
creatures flashed and
shimmered there—
lost images
fadingly remembered.
Swiftly descended
into canyon of cold
nightgreen emptiness.
Freefalling, weightless
as in dreams of
wingless flight,
plunged through infra-
space and came to

the dead ship,
carcass that swarmed with
voracious life.
Angelfish, their
lively blue and
yellow prised from
darkness by the
flashlight's beam,
thronged her portholes.
Moss of bryozoans
blurred, obscured her
metal. Snappers,
gold groupers explored her,
fearless of bubbling
manfish. I entered
the wreck, awed by her silence,
feeling more keenly
the iron cold.
With flashlight probing
fogs of water
saw the sad slow
dance of gilded
chairs, the ectoplasmic
swirl of garments,
drowned instruments
of bouyancy,
drunken shoes. Then
livid gesturings,
eldritch hide and
seek of laughing
faces. I yearned to
find those hidden
ones, to fling aside
the mask and call to them,
yield to rapturous
whisperings, have
done with self and
every dinning
vain complexity.
Yet in languid
frenzy strove, as
one freezing fights off
sleep desiring sleep;

strove against the
cancelling arms that
suddenly surrounded
me, fled the numbing
kisses that I craved.
Reflex of life-wish?
Respirator's brittle
belling? Swam from
the ship somehow;
somehow began the
measured rise.

1960

DUDLEY RANDALL

Booker T. and W. E. B.

(BOOKER T. WASHINGTON AND W. E. B. DuBOIS)

"It seems to me," said Booker T.,
"It shows a mighty lot of cheek
To study chemistry and Greek
When Mister Charlie needs a hand
To hoe the cotton on his land,
And when Miss Ann looks for a cook,
Why stick your nose inside a book?"

"I don't agree," said W. E. B.
"If I should have the drive to seek
Knowledge of chemistry or Greek,
I'll do it. Charles and Miss can look
Another place for hand or cook.
Some men rejoice in skill of hand,
And some in cultivating land,
But there are others who maintain
The right to cultivate the brain."

"It seems to me," said Booker T.,
"That all you folks have missed the boat
Who shout about the right to vote,
And spend vain days and sleepless nights
In uproar over civil rights.
Just keep your mouths shut, do not grouse,
But work, and save, and buy a house."

"I don't agree," said W. E. B.
"For what can poverty avail
If dignity and justice fail?
Unless you help to make the laws,
They'll steal your house with trumped-up clause.

A rope's as tight, a fire as hot,
No matter how much cash you've got.
Speak soft, and try your little plan,
But as for me, I'll be a man."

"It seems to me," said Booker T.—

"I don't agree,"
Said W. E. B.

1948

The Southern Road

There the black river, boundary to hell,
And here the iron bridge, the ancient car,
And grim conductor, who with surly yell
Forbids white soldiers where the black ones are.
And I re-live the enforced avatar
Of shuddering journey to a dark abode,
Made by my sires before another war;
And I set forth upon the southern road.

To a land where shadowed songs like flowers swell
And where the earth is scarlet as a scar
Friezed by the bleeding lash that fell (O fell)
Upon my fathers' flesh. O far, far, far
And deep my blood has drenched it. None can bar
My birthright to the loveliness bestowed
Upon this country haughty as a star.
And I set forth upon the southern road.

This darkness and these mountains loom a spell
Of peak-roofed town where yearning steeples soar
And the holy chanting of a bell
Shakes human incense on the throbbing air
Where bonfires blaze and quivering bodies char.
Whose hair crisped black like cotton, and fiercely glowed?
I know it; and my entrails melt like tar
And I set forth upon the southern road.

O fertile hillsides where my fathers are,
From which my griefs like troubled streams have flowed.

I have to love you, though they sweep me far.
And I set forth upon the southern road.

1948

Legacy: My South

When desperate nightmare rapts me to this land
Lit by a bloody moon, red on the hills,
Red in the valleys? Why am I compelled
To walk where dead men walked, to feel their pain,
To shed my tears where blood and tears have flowed?
Compulsion of the blood and of the moon
Transports me. I was molded from this clay.
My blood must ransom all the blood shed here,
My tears redeem the tears. Cripples and monsters
Are here. My flesh must make them whole and hale.
I am the sacrifice.

See where the halt
Attempt again and again to cross a line
Their minds have drawn, but fear snatches them back
Though health and joy wait on the other side.
And there another locks himself in a room
And throws away the key. A ragged scarecrow
Cackles an antique lay, and cries himself
Lord of the world. A naked plowman falls
Famished upon the plow, and overhead
A lean bird circles

1948

Ballad of Birmingham

(ON THE BOMBING OF A CHURCH IN
BIRMINGHAM, ALABAMA, 1963)

"Mother dear, may I go downtown
Instead of out to play,
And march the streets of Birmingham
In a Freedom March today?"

"No, baby, no, you may not go,
For the dogs are fierce and wild,

And clubs and hoses, guns and jail
Aren't good for a little child."

"But, mother, I won't be alone.
Other children will go with me,
And march the streets of Birmingham
To make our country free."

"No, baby, no, you may not go,
For I fear those guns will fire.
But you may go to church instead
And sing in the children's choir."

She has combed and brushed her night-dark hair,
And bathed rose petal sweet,
And drawn white gloves on her small brown hands,
And white shoes on her feet.

The mother smiled to know her child
Was in the sacred place,
But that smile was the last smile
To come upon her face.

For when she heard the explosion,
Her eyes grew wet and wild.
She raced through the streets of Birmingham
Calling for her child.

She clawed through bits of glass and brick,
Then lifted out a shoe.
"O, here's the shoe my baby wore,
But, baby, where are you?"

1963

MARGARET WALKER

For My People

For my people everywhere singing their slave songs repeatedly: their dirges and their ditties and their blues and jubilees, praying their prayers nightly to an unknown god, bending their knees humbly to an unseen power;

For my people lending their strength to the years, to the gone years and the now years and the maybe years, washing ironing cooking scrubbing sewing mending hoeing plowing digging planting pruning patching dragging alone never gaining never reaping never knowing and never understanding;

For my playmates in the clay and dust and sand of Alabama backyards playing baptizing and preaching and doctor and jail and soldier and school and mama and cooking and playhouse and concert and store and hair and Miss Choomby and company;

For the cramped bewildered years we went to school to learn to know the reasons why and the answers to and the people who and the places where and the days when, in memory of the bitter hours when we discovered we were black and poor and small and different and nobody cared and nobody wondered and nobody understood;

For the boys and girls who grew in spite of these things to be man and woman, to laugh and dance and sing and play and drink their wine and religion and success, to marry their playmates and bear children and then die of consumption and anemia and lynching;

For my people thronging 47th Street in Chicago and Lenox Avenue in New York and Rampart Street in New Orleans, lost disinherited dispossessed and happy people filling the cabarets and taverns and other people's pockets needing bread and shoes and milk and land and money and something—something all our own;

For my people walking blindly spreading joy, losing time being lazy, sleeping when hungry, shouting when burdened, drinking when hopeless, tied and shackled and tangled among ourselves by the unseen creatures who tower over us omnisciently and laugh;

For my people blundering and groping and floundering in the dark of churches and schools and clubs and societies, associations and councils and committees and conventions, distressed and disturbed and deceived and devoured by money-hungry glory-craving leeches, preyed on by facile force of state and fad and novelty, by false prophet and holy believer;

For my people standing staring trying to fashion a better way from confusion, from hypocrisy and misunderstanding, trying to fashion a world that will hold all the people, all the faces, all the adams and eves and their countless generations;

Let a new earth rise. Let another world be born. Let a bloody peace be written in the sky. Let a second generation full of courage issue forth; let a people loving freedom come to growth. Let a beauty full of healing and a strength of final clenching be the pulsing in our spirits and our blood. Let the martial songs be written, let the dirges disappear. Let a race of men now rise and take control.

Molly Means

Old Molly Means was a hag and a witch;
Chile of the devil, the dark, and sitch.
Her heavy hair hung thick in ropes
And her blazing eyes was black as pitch.
Imp at three and wench at 'leben
She counted her husbands to the number seben.

O Molly, Molly, Molly Means
There goes the ghost of Molly Means.

Some say she was born with a veil on her face
So she could look through unnatchal space
Through the future and through the past
And charm a body or an evil place
And every man could well despise
The evil look in her coal black eyes.
Old Molly, Molly, Molly Means
Dark is the ghost of Molly Means.

And when the tale begun to spread
Of evil and of holy dread:
Her black-hand arts and her evil powers
How she cast her spells and called the dead,
The younguns was afraid at night
And the farmers feared their crops would blight.
Old Molly, Molly, Molly Means
Cold is the ghost of Molly Means.

Then one dark day she put a spell
On a young gal-bride just come to dwell
In the lane just down from Molly's shack
And when her husband came riding back
His wife was barking like a dog
And on all fours like a common hog.
O Molly, Molly, Molly Means
Where is the ghost of Molly Means?

The neighbors come and they went away
And said she'd die before break of day
But her husband held her in his arms
And swore he'd break the wicked charms;
He'd search all up and down the land
And turn the spell on Molly's hand.
O Molly, Molly, Molly Means
Sharp is the ghost of Molly Means.

So he rode all day and he rode all night
And at the dawn he came in sight
Of a man who said he could move the spell
And cause the awful thing to dwell

On Molly Means, to bark and bleed
Till she died at the hands of her evil deed.
Old Molly, Molly, Molly Means
This is the ghost of Molly Means.

Sometimes at night through the shadowy trees
She rides along on a winter breeze.
You can hear her holler and whine and cry.
Her voice is thin and her moan is high,
And her cackling laugh or her barking cold
Bring terror to the young and old.
O Molly, Molly, Molly Means
Lean is the ghost of Molly Means.

We Have Been Believers

We have been believers believing in the black gods of an old land, believing in the secrets of the seeress and the magic of the charmers and the power of the devil's evil ones.

And in the white gods of a new land we have been believers believing in the mercy of our masters and the beauty of our brothers, believing in the conjure of the humble and the faithful and the pure.

Neither the slavers' whip nor the lynchers' rope nor the bayonet could kill our black belief. In our hunger we beheld the welcome table and in our nakedness the glory of a long white robe. We have been believers in the new Jerusalem.

We have been believers feeding greedy grinning gods, like a Moloch demanding our sons and our daughters, our strength and our wills and our spirits of pain. We have been believers, silent and stolid and stubborn and strong.

We have been believers yielding substance for the world. With our hands have we fed a people and out of our strength have they wrung the necessities of a nation. Our song has filled the twilight and our hope has heralded the dawn.

Now we stand ready for the touch of one fiery iron, for the cleansing breath of many molten truths, that the eyes of the blind may see and the ears of the deaf may hear and the tongues of the people be filled with living fire.

Where are our gods that they leave us asleep? Surely the priests and the preachers and the powers will hear. Surely now that our hands are empty and our hearts too full to pray they will understand. Surely the sires of the people will send us a sign.

We have been believers believing in our burdens and our demigods too long. Now the needy no longer weep and pray; the long-suffering arise, and our fists bleed against the bars with a strange insistency.

Lineage

My grandmothers were strong.
They followed plows and bent to toil.
They moved through fields sowing seed.
They touched earth and grain grew.
They were full of sturdiness and singing.
My grandmothers were strong.

My grandmothers are full of memories
Smelling of soap and onions and wet clay
With veins rolling roughly over quick hands
They have many clean words to say.
My grandmothers were strong.
Why am I not as they?

Childhood

When I was a child I knew red miners
dressed raggedly and wearing carbide lamps.
I saw them come down red hills to their camps
dyed with red dust from old Ishkooda mines.
Night after night I met them on the roads,
or on the streets in town I caught their glance;
the swing of dinner buckets in their hands,
and grumbling undermining all their words.

I also lived in low cotton country
where moonlight hovered over ripe haystacks,
or stumps of trees, and croppers' rotting shacks
with famine, terror, flood, and plague near by;
where sentiment and hatred still held sway
and only bitter land was washed away.

GWENDOLYN BROOKS

the mother

Abortions will not let you forget.
You remember the children you got that you did not get,
The damp small pulps with a little or with no hair,
The singers and workers that never handled the air.
You will never neglect or beat
Them, or silence or buy with a sweet.
You will never wind up the sucking-thumb
Or scuttle off ghosts that come.
You will never leave them, controlling your luscious sigh,
Return for a snack of them, with gobbling mother-eye.

I have heard in the voices of the wind the voices of my dim killed
children.
I have contracted. I have eased
My dim dears at the breasts they could never suck.
I have said, Sweets, if I sinned, if I seized
Your luck
And your lives from your unfinished reach,
If I stole your births and your names,
Your straight baby tears and your games,
Your stilted or lovely loves, your tumults, your marriages, aches,
and your deaths,
If I poisoned the beginnings of your breaths,
Believe that even in my deliberateness I was not deliberate.
Though why should I whine,
Whine that the crime was other than mine?—
Since anyhow you are dead.
Or rather, or instead,
You were never made.
But that too, I am afraid,
Is faulty: oh, what shall I say, how is the truth to be said?
You were born, you had body, you died.
It is just that you never giggled or planned or cried.

Believe me, I loved you all.
Believe me, I knew you, though faintly, and I loved, I loved you
All.

c. 1945

the preacher: ruminates behind the sermon

I think it must be lonely to be God.
Nobody loves a master. No. Despite
The bright hosannas, bright dear-Lords, and bright
Determined reverence of Sunday eyes.

Picture Jehovah striding through the hall
Of His importance, creatures running out
From servant-corners to acclaim, to shout
Appreciation of His merit's glare.

But who walks with Him?—dares to take His arm,
To slap Him on the shoulder, tweak His ear,
Buy Him a Coca-Cola or a beer,
Pooh-pooh His politics, call Him a fool?

Perhaps—who knows?—He tires of looking down.
Those eyes are never lifted. Never straight.
Perhaps sometimes He tires of being great
In solitude. Without a hand to hold.

c. 1945

from the children of the poor

What shall I give my children? who are poor,
Who are adjudged the leastwise of the land,
Who are my sweetest lepers, who demand
No velvet and no velvety velour;
But who have begged me for a brisk contour,
Crying that they are quasi, contraband
Because unfinished, graven by a hand
Less than angelic, admirable or sure.
My hand is stuffed with mode, design, device.
But I lack access to my proper stone.
And plenitude of plan shall not suffice
Nor grief nor love shall be enough alone

— to carve a statue. — to delineate clearly

[illegible] COVENANT
UNITED CHURCH OF CHRIST
March [illegible], 1998

Gathering Music

Gathering Song - "Jesus Savior, Pilot Me"

Gathering - The Amistad Story

Opening Song - "We Shall Overcome"

Reading - from Robert Hayden's "[illegible]"

Song - "[illegible] Who See Light"

Offering and Dedicating Our [illegible]

Song - [illegible]

To ratify my little halves who bear
Across an autumn freezing everywhere.

c. 1949

The Bean Eaters

They eat beans mostly, this old yellow pair.
Dinner is a casual affair.
Plain chipware on a plain and creaking wood,
Tin flatware.

Two who are Mostly Good.
Two who have lived their day,
But keep on putting on their clothes
And putting things away.

And remembering . . .
Remembering, with twinklings and twinges,
As they lean over the beans in their rented back room that is full of beads and receipts and dolls and cloths, tobacco crumbs, vases and fringes.

c. 1959

We Real Cool

THE POOL PLAYERS.
SEVEN AT THE GOLDEN SHOVEL.

We real cool. We
Left school. We

Lurk late. We
Strike straight. We

Sing sin. We
Thin gin. We

Jazz June. We
Die soon.

c. 1959

The Chicago Defender Sends a Man to Little Rock

FALL, 1957

In Little Rock the people bear
Babes, and comb and part their hair
And watch the want ads, put repair
To roof and latch. While wheat toast burns
A woman waters multiferns.

Time upholds or overturns
The many, tight, and small concerns.

In Little Rock the people sing
Sunday hymns like anything,
Through Sunday pomp and polishing.

And after testament and tunes,
Some soften Sunday afternoons
With lemon tea and Lorna Doones.

I forecast
And I believe
Come Christmas Little Rock will cleave
To Christmas tree and trifle, weave,
From laugh and tinsel, texture fast.

In Little Rock is baseball; Barcarolle.
That hotness in July . . . the uniformed figures raw and implacable
And not intellectual,
Batting the hotness or clawing the suffering dust.
The Open Air Concert, on the special twilight green . . . .
When Beethoven is brutal or whispers to lady-like air.
Blanket-sitters are seldom, as Johann troubles to lean
To tell them what to mean . . . .

There is love, too, in Little Rock. Soft women softly
Opening themselves in kindness,
Or, pitying one's blindness,
Awaiting one's pleasure
In azure
Glory with anguished rose at the root . . . .

To wash away old semi-discomfitures.
They re-teach purple and unsullen blue.
The wispy soils go. And uncertain
Half-havings have they clarified to sures.

In Little Rock they know
Not answering the telephone is a way of rejecting life,
That it is our business to be bothered, is our business
To cherish bores or boredom, be polite
To lies and love and many-faceted fuzziness.

I scratch my head, massage the hate-I-had.
I blink across my prim and pencilled pad.
The saga I was sent for is not down.
Because there is a puzzle in this town.
The biggest News I do not dare
Telegraph to the Editor's chair:
"They are like people everywhere."

The angry Editor would reply
In hundred harryings of Why.

And true, they are hurling spittle, rock,
Garbage and fruit in Little Rock.
And I saw coiling storm-a-writhe
On bright madonnas. And a scythe
Of men harassing brownish girls.
(The bows and barrettes in the curls
And braids declined away from joy.)

I saw a bleeding brownish boy . . . .

The lariat lynch-wish I deplored.

The loveliest lynchee was our Lord.

c. 1960

The Lovers of the Poor

arrive. The Ladies from the Ladies' Betterment League
Arrive in the afternoon, the late light slanting

In diluted gold bars across the boulevard brag
Of proud, seamed faces with mercy and murder hinting
Here, there, interrupting, all deep and debonair,
The pink paint on the innocence of fear;
Walk in a gingerly manner up the hall.
Cutting with knives served by their softest care,
Served by their love, so barbarously fair.
Whose mothers taught: You'd better not be cruel!
You had better not throw stones upon the wrens!
Herein they kiss and coddle and assault
Anew and dearly in the innocence
With which they baffle nature. Who are full,
Sleek, tender-clad, fit, fiftyish, a-glow, all
Sweetly abortive, hinting at fat fruit,
Judge it high time that fiftyish fingers felt
Beneath the lovelier planes of enterprise.
To resurrect. To moisten with milky chill.
To be a random hitching-post or plush.
To be, for wet eyes, random and handy hem.
    Their guild is giving money to the poor.
The worthy poor. The very very worthy
And beautiful poor. Perhaps just not too swarthy?
Perhaps just not too dirty nor too dim
Nor—passionate. In truth, what they could wish
Is—something less than derelict or dull.
Not staunch enough to stab, though, gaze for gaze!
God shield them sharply from the beggar-bold!
The noxious needy ones whose battle's bald
Nonetheless for being voiceless, hits one down.
    But it's all so bad! and entirely too much for them.
The stench; the urine, cabbage, and dead beans,
Dead porridges of assorted dusty grains,
The old smoke, *heavy* diapers, and, they're told,
Something called chitterlings. The darkness. Drawn
Darkness, or dirty light. The soil that stirs.
The soil that looks the soil of centuries.
And for that matter the *general* oldness. Old
Wood. Old marble. Old tile. Old old old.
Not homekind Oldness! Not Lake Forest, Glencoe.
Nothing is sturdy, nothing is majestic,
There is no quiet drama, no rubbed glaze, no
Unkillable infirmity of such
A tasteful turn as lately they have left,

Glencoe, Lake Forest, and to which their cars
Must presently restore them. When they're done
With dullards and distortions of this fistic
Patience of the poor and put-upon.
        They've never seen such a make-do-ness as
Newspaper rugs before! In this, this "flat,"
Their hostess is gathering up the oozed, the rich
Rugs of the morning (tattered! the bespattered . . . .)
Readies to spread clean rugs for afternoon.
Here is a scene for you. The Ladies look,
In horror, behind a substantial citizeness
Whose trains clank out across her swollen heart.
Who, arms akimbo, almost fills a door.
All tumbling children, quilts dragged to the floor
And tortured thereover, potato peelings, soft-
Eyed kitten, hunched-up, haggard, to-be-hurt.
        Their League is allotting largesse to the Lost.
But to put their clean, their pretty money, to put
Their money collected from delicate rose-fingers
Tipped with their hundred flawless rose-nails seems . . .
        They own Spode, Lowestoft, candelabra,
Mantels, and hostess gowns, and sunburst clocks,
Turtle soup, Chippendale, red satin "hangings,"
Aubussons and Hattie Carnegie. They Winter
In Palm Beach; cross the Water in June; attend,
When suitable, the nice Art Institute;
Buy the right books in the best bindings; saunter
On Michigan, Easter mornings, in sun or wind.
Oh Squalor! This sick four-story hulk, this fibre
With fissures everywhere! Why, what are bringings
Of loathe-love largesse? What shall peril hungers
So old old, what shall flatter the desolate?
Tin can, blocked fire escape and chitterling
And swaggering seeking youth and the puzzled wreckage
Of the middle passage, and urine and stale shames
And, again, the porridges of the underslung
And children children children. Heavens! That
Was a rat, surely, off there, in the shadows? Long
And long-tailed? Gray? The Ladies from the Ladies'
Betterment League agree it will be better
To achieve the outer air that rights and steadies,
To hie to a house that does not holler, to ring
Bells elsetime, better presently to cater

To no more Possibilities, to get
Away. Perhaps the money can be posted.
Perhaps they two may choose another Slum!
Some serious sooty half-unhappy home!—
Where loathe-love likelier may be invested.
            Keeping their scented bodies in the center
Of the hall as they walk down the hysterical hall,
They allow their lovely skirts to graze no wall,
Are off at what they manage of a canter,
And, resuming all the clues of what they were,
Try to avoid inhaling the laden air.

c. 1960

MARGARET DANNER

I'll Walk the Tightrope

I'll walk the tightrope that's been stretched for me,
and though a wrinkled forehead, perplexed why,
will accompany me, I'll delicately
step along. For if I stop to sigh
at the earth-propped stride
of others, I will fall. I must balance high
without a parasol to tide
a faltering step, without a net below,
without a balance stick to guide.

1950

The Elevator Man Adheres to Form

I am reminded, by the tan man who wings
the elevator, of Rococo art. His ways
are undulating waves that shepherd and swing
us cupid-like from floor to floor.

He sweethearts us
with polished pleasantries; gallantly
flourishing us up and up. No casual "Hi's" from him.

His greetings, Godspeedings, display his Ph.D.
aplomb, and I should feel like a cherubim,
be fleur-de-lis and pastel-shell-like, but

instead, I vision other tan and deeper much than tan
early-Baroque-like men, who (seeing themselves still strutlessly
groping, winding down subterranean

grottoes of injustice, down dark spirals) feel
with such tortuous, smoked-stone greyed intensity
that they exhale a hurricane of gargoyles, then reel

into it. I see these others boggling in their misery
and wish this elevator artisan would fill his flourishing form
with warmth for them and turn his lettered zeal
toward lifting them above their crippling storm.

1951

Far From Africa: Four Poems

"are you beautiful still?"

1. GARNISHING THE AVIARY

Our moulting days are in their twilight stage.
These lengthy dreaded suns of draggling plumes.
These days of moods that swiftly alternate between

The former preen (ludicrous now) and a downcast rage
Or crestfallen lag, are fading out. The initial bloom;
Exotic, dazzling in its indigo, tangerine

Splendor; this rare, conflicting coat had to be shed.
Our drooping feathers turn all shades. We spew
This unamicable aviary, gag upon the worm, and fling

Our loosening quills. We make a riotous spread
Upon the dust and mire that beds us. We do not shoo
So quickly; but the shades of the pinfeathers resulting
From this chaotic push, though still exotic,
Blend in more easily with those on the wings
Of the birds surrounding them; garnishing
The aviary, burnishing this zoo.

2. DANCE OF THE ABAKWETA

Imagine what Mrs. Haessler would say
If she could see the Watusi youth dance
Their well-versed initiation. At first glance
As they bend to an invisible barre
You would know that she had designed their costumes.

For though they were made of pale beige bamboo straw

Their lines were the classic tutu. Nothing varied.
Each was cut short at the thigh and carried
High to a degree of right angles. Nor was there a flaw
In their leotards. Made of leopard skin or the hide

Of a goat, or the Gauguin-colored Okapi's striped coat
They were cut in her reverenced "tradition."
She would have approved their costumes and positions.
And since neither Iceland nor Africa is too remote
For her vision she would have wanted to form

A "traditional" ballet. Swan Lake, Scheherazade or
(After seeing their incredible leaps)
Les Orientales. Imagine the exotic sweep
Of such a ballet, and from the way the music pours

Over these dancers (this tinkling of bells, talking
Of drums, and twanging of tan, sandalwood harps)
From this incomparable music, Mrs. Haessler of Vassar can
Glimpse strains of Tchaikovsky, Chopin
To accompany her undeviatingly sharp
"Traditional" ballet. I am certain that if she could
Tutor these potential protégés, as
Quick as Aladdin rubbing his lamp, she would.

3. THE VISIT OF THE PROFESSOR OF AESTHETICS

To see you standing in the sagging bookstore door
So filled me with chagrin that suddenly you seemed as
Pink and white to me as a newborn, hairless mouse. For

I had hoped to delight you at home. Be a furl
Of faint perfume and Vienna's cordlike lace.
To shine my piano till a shimmer of mother-of-pearl

Embraced it. To pleasantly surprise you with the grace
That transcends my imitation and much worn
"Louis XV" couch. To display my Cathedrals and ballets.

To plunge you into Africa through my nude
Zulu Prince, my carvings from Benin, forlorn
Treasures garnered by much sacrifice of food.

I had hoped to delight you, for more
Rare than the seven-year bloom of my
Chinese spiderweb fern is a mind like yours

That concedes my fetish for this substance
Of your trade. And I had planned to prove
Your views of me correct at even every chance

Encounter. But you surprised me. And the store which
Had shown promise until you came, arose
Like a child gone wild when company comes or a witch

At Hallowe'en. The floor, just swept and mopped,
Was persuaded by the northlight to deny it.
The muddy rag floor rugs hunched and flopped

Away from the tears in the linoleum that I wanted
Them to hide. The drapes that I had pleated
In clear orchid and peach feverishly flaunted

Their greasiest folds like a banner.
The books who had been my friends, retreated—
Became as shy as the proverbial poet in manner

And hid their better selves. All glow had been deleted
By the dirt. And I felt that you whose god is grace
Could find no semblance of it here. And unaware

That you were scrubbing, you scrubbed your hands.
Wrung and scrubbed your long white fingers. Scrubbed
Them as you smiled and I lowered my eyes from despair.

4. ETTA MOTEN'S ATTIC

(Filled with mementos of African journeys)

It was as if Gauguin
had upset a huge paint pot
of his incomparable tangerine,

splashing wherever my startled eyes ran
here and there, and at my very hand on
masques and paintings and carvings not seen

here before, spilling straight as a stripe
spun geometrically in a Nbeble rug
flung over an ebony chair,

or dripping round as a band on a type
of bun the Watusi warriors
make of their pompadoured hair,

splashing high as a sunbird or fly moving
over a frieze of mahogany trees,
or splotching out from low underneath as a root,

shimmering bright as a ladybug grooving
a green bed of moss, sparkling as a beetle,
a bee, shockingly dotting the snoot

of an ape or the nape of its neck or as clue
to its navel, stamping a Zulu's
intriguing masque, tipping

the lips of a chief of Ashantis who
was carved to his stool so he'd sit
there forever and never fear a slipping

of rule or command, dyeing the skirt
(all askew) that wouldn't stay put on the
Pygmy in spite of his real leather belt,

quickening and charming till we felt the bloom
of veldt and jungle flow through the room.

1951

NAOMI LONG MADGETT

Native

Down the unspun swerve of trackless weeds
I travel unaware.
Propelled by sudden vengeances of seeds
Of anywhere
Whose hues I never learned nor whose design.
Unmindful of intent,
I wander where the knowing roots entwine
The innocent,
And suck the pungent juice into my vein,
And do not question why.
Except no definition to explain
Or deify.
For blessed or damned, inherent in my lust
And native to my need
Is this same potent urgency that dust
Conveys to seed.

1957

Mortality

This is the surest death
Of all the deaths I know.
The one that halts the breath,
The one that falls with snow
Are nothing but a peace
Before the second zone,
For Aprils never cease
To resurrect their own,
And in my very veins
Flows blood as old as Eve.
The smallest cell contains
Its privileged reprieve.

But vultures recognize
This single mortal thing
And watch with hungry eyes
When hope starts staggering.

1957

Midway

I've come this far to freedom and I won't turn back.
I'm climbing to the highway from my old dirt track.
    I'm coming and I'm going
    And I'm stretching and I'm growing
And I'll reap what I've been sowing or my skin's not black.

I've prayed and slaved and waited and I've sung my song.
You've bled me and you've starved me but I've still grown strong.
    You've lashed me and you've treed me
    And you've everything but freed me
But in time you'll know you need me and it won't be long.

I've seen the daylight breaking high above the bough.
I've found my destination and I've made my vow;
    So whether you abhor me
    Or deride me or ignore me,
Mighty mountains loom before me and I won't stop now.

1959

The Race Question

(For one whose fame depends on keeping The Problem a problem)

Would it please you if I strung my tears
In pearls for you to wear?
Would you like a gift of my hands' endless beating
Against old bars?

This time I can forget my Otherness,
Silence my drums of discontent awhile
And listen to the stars.

Wait in the shadows if you choose.
Stand alert to catch
The thunder and first sprinkle of unrest
Your insufficiency demands.
But you will find no comfort.
I will not feed your hunger with my blood
Nor crown your nakedness
With jewels of my elegant pain.

1963

GLORIA C. ODEN

Review from Staten Island

The skyline of New York does not excite me
(ferrying towards it) as mountains do in snow-steeped
hostility to sun.
There is something in the view—spewed up from water
to pure abandonment in air—
that snakes my spine with cold
and mouse-tracks over my heart.

Strewn across the meet of wave and wind, it seems
the incompleted play of some helter-skeltering child whose
hegira (as all
our circles go) has not yet led him back, but will, ripe
with that ferocious glee which
can boot these building-blocks
to earth, then heel under.

One gets used to dying living. Growth is an
end to many things—even the rose disposes of summer—
but still I
wince at being there when the relentless foot kicks down;
and the tides come roaring over
to pool within
the unlearned depths of me.

The Carousel

"I turned from side to side, from image to image to put you down."
—LOUISE BOGAN

An empty carousel in a deserted park
rides me round and round,

forth and back
from end to beginning,
like the tail that drives the dog.

I cannot see:
sight focuses shadow where once
pleased scenery,
and in this whirl of space
only the indefinite is constant.

This is the way of grief:
spinning in the rhythm of memories
that will not let you up
or down,
but keeps you grinding through
a granite air.

". . . As When Emotion Too Far Exceeds its Cause"

—ELIZABETH BISHOP

You probably could put their names to them.
The birds, I mean.
Though I have often watched their rushing
about the upper air
(deliberate as subway riders
who are not anywhere near
so orderly),
I have never stopped to inquire the name
of that one or another.
Still, I did take time
to observe them in their dips and circles
and jet-propelled ascendancies.

It's all in the wings I am told.
That could be said of angels.
I grant it may be true;
undoubtedly is,
since my informants know more

than I. But,
still, I wonder
and harbor fear that we all are wrong
to think that birds do fly.
What if, one day, upon the ground with us
we found them;
their wings unable to lift them
anywhere except into a deeper stratum
of despair.
Would it all be a matter of wings?
Does flight depend upon such feathered things?

Or is it air? I do not trust the stuff.
Seeing the birds beating about in it,
I want to say, "Take care; and
don't believe in what it seems you do!"
Sometimes I stray across a small one

I should have said it to;
one who for all his modern design
to sweep and arch the atmosphere
had plummeted, instead, to earth
and worms that do not care about horizons.
If I retreat,
too shocked to cast the benediction
of a single leaf,
understand why:
I know the error in invisible support;
in love's celestial venturing
I, too, once trusted air
that plunged me down.
Yes, I!

The Map

My rug is red. My couch, whereon I deal
in dreams with truths I never live, is brown;
a shading more intense than that by my
skin declared. Richer it is, too, than of
any of the eight clear hues coloring

my wide, world map soldiering the white wall
there behind it. This map is of the world.
It says so. In type 1/2" high: WORLD;
and with what I know of maps I do, in
deed, believe it—though over it, in type
now smaller by one-half, I read the word
"COSMOPOLITAN," and over that in
type yet smaller by one-half, these gentile
modifiers "RAND McNALLY."

The seas
square off in blue. Or, ought the word be "sea"?
Uniformly bright, planed by a tone so
mild you might suppose the North Sea twinned the
South and that the Moskenstraumen was (for
the most part) Poe (quote) *Sailing directions*
for the northwest and north coast of Norway
(unquote) to the contrary; seven diminishes
to one, where none arrests attention.

Not
so the land. Flowering forth as spring in
May will settle down to deed, it woos us
with such yellows, pinks and greens as would, I'm
sure, lure the most selective butterfly;
and each trim hue is sized the living room
of nations.

America (U. S.) is
daffodil; Canada carnation; while
leaflike as an elephant ear, Greenland
hangs indifferent to those arctic winds parching
the cell-like bounds of Russia (here halved and
showing both to the left and right of this
our hemisphere—indeed, as is a good
part of the orient split, some even
to doubling appearance.)

Europe (also)
lies fragmented; though from nature's—not the
mapmaker's—division. Ireland off-
set from England, offset from France (feigning
oasis besides the rot-brown fill to

Germany) supplies one awkward revel
of abstraction as that gross bud of Spain
(with Portugal) patterns another; not
to mention Italy's invasion of
the sea.

Norway, Sweden, much as giraffes
must bend, towards Denmark group in restricted
covenant; yet, though this canvas—Europe—
at its center holds, such unity rests
more upon imagination than that,
let's say, of Africa islanded in
those deeper latitudes.

There, it is the
green (again) I think. Incandescent flood
like the dead reckoning of spring; at four
points edging sea; it seems a fever of
the mind within that broad head housed (it shapes
—Africa—a head to me!) which in its
course will blaze the length of continent as
now it fires breadth.

And who will say it
won't? Not the mapmaker, surely, who must
exact truth. Not I, high hoisting same to,
state whirlwind. Will you, because you might not
particularly care to see it so?

TED JOANS

The Truth

IF YOU SHOULD SEE A M A N
walking down a crowded
street
talking
ALOUD
TO HIMSELF
DON'T RUN
IN THE
OPPOSITE DIRECTION
BUT RUN
TOWARD HIM
for he is a
POET
You have NOTHING to
FEAR
FROM THE
POET
BUT THE
TRUTH

For Me Again

I'VE SEEN MY MOTHER AGAIN MORE YEARS THAN TEN
HAVE PASSED BY
SHE STILL FAT LIKE THE SUN COOKING OLD SMELLY SOUL
FOODS FOR ME AGAIN

MORE YEARS THAN TEN HAVE PASSED US BY SEEING/HEARING/
FEELING/SILENTLY TOGETHER
WE CRY MY MOTHER AND I She still wise and warm for me again
This woman/my mother This woman/MY FRIEND

Why Try?

And she was brown
And she always dressed and wore brown
And she had a fine brown body
And she had two beautiful brown eyes
And she would sit in the Beat Cafe
on her brown behind on a hard brown bench
and listen to brown sounds entertain her brown thoughts
And she would often double cross her brown legs
And reveal her beautiful brown pleasing knees
And as she sat in the Beat Cafe on her brown behind on the hard
brown bench
And listening to brown sounds coming from entertainers of
brown bohemia
I saw a young white girl throw away her brand
new jar of
suntan lotion and sigh: WHY TRY?

Lester Young

Sometimes he was cool like an eternal
blue flame burning in the old Kansas
City nunnery
Sometimes he was happy 'til he'd think
about his birth place and its blood
stained clay hills and crow-filled trees
Most times he was blowin' on the wonderful
tenor sax of his, preachin' in very cool
tones, shouting only to remind you of
a certain point in his blue messages
He was our president as well as the minister
of soul stirring Jazz, he knew what he

blew, and he did what a prez should do,
wail, wail, wail. There were many of
them to follow him and most of them were
fair—but they never spoke so eloquently
in so a far out funky air.
Our prez done died, he know'd this would come
but death has only booked him, alongside
Bird, Art Tatum, and other heavenly wailers.
Angels of Jazz—they don't die—they live
they live—in hipsters like you and I

The .38

i hear the man downstairs slapping the hell out of his stupid
wife again
i hear him push and shove her around the overcrowded room
i hear her scream and beg for mercy
i hear him tell her *there is no mercy*
i hear the blows as they land on her beautiful body
i hear her screams and pleas
i hear glasses and pots and pans falling
i hear fleeing from the room
i hear them running up the stairs
i hear her outside MY DOOR!
i hear him coming toward her outside MY DOOR!!
i hear her banging on MY DOOR!!!
i hear him bang her head on MY DOOR!
I HEAR HIM TRYING TO DRAG HER AWAY FROM MY DOOR
i hear her hands desperate on my door knob
i hear him bang her head against my door
i hear him drag her away from my door
i hear him drag her down the stairs
i hear her head bounce from step to step
i hear him drag that beautiful body
i hear them again in their room
THEN i hear a loud slap across her face (i guess)
i hear her groan . . . . then
i hear the eerie silence
i hear him open the top drawer of his bureau the .38 lives
there!!!

i hear the fast beat of my heart

i hear the drops of perspiration fall from my brow
i hear him yell: I WARNED YOU!!!
i hear him pull her limp body across their overcrowded room
i hear the springs of their bed creak from the weight of her beautiful
body
i hear him say DAMN YOU, I WARNED YOU, AND NOW IT'S
TOO LATE
THEN I HEAR THE LOUD REPORT OF THE THIRTY EIGHT
CALIBER REVOLVER!!!
i hear it again and again the Smith & Wessen
i hear the BANG BANG BANG BANG of four death-dealing
bullets!
i hear my heart beat faster and louder . . . . and then
again
i hear the eerie silence
i hear him walk out of their overcrowded room
i hear him walk up the steps
i hear him come toward MY DOOR!
i hear his hand on my door knob
i hear my door knob click
i hear the door slowly open
i hear him step into my room
i hear him standing there/breathing heavy/and taking aim
I HEAR THE CLICK OF THE THIRTY EIGHT JUST BEFORE
THE FIRING PIN HITS THE DEATH-DEALING BULLET!!
I HEAR THE LOUD BLAST OF THE POWDER EXPLODING IN
THE CHAMBER OF THE .38!
I HEAR THE HEAVY LEAD NOSE OF THE BULLET SWIFTLY
CUTTING ITS WAY THROUGH THE BARREL OF THE .38!
I HEAR IT EMERGE OUT INTO SPACE FROM THE .38!
I HEAR THE BULLET OF DEATH FLYING TOWARD MY HEAD
THE .38!!
I HEAR IT COMING FASTER THAN SOUND THE .38!

I HEAR IT COMING CLOSER TO MY SWEATY FOREHEAD
THE .38!
I HEAR AND NOW I CAN SEE IT THE .38!
I HEAR ITS WEIRD WHISTLE THE .38!

I HEAR IT JUST ONE INCH FROM MY HEAD THE .38!!

I HEAR IT GIVE OFF A LITTLE STEAMLIKE NOISE
WHEN IT CUTS THROUGH MY SWEAT THE .38!!!

I HEAR IT SINGE MY SKIN AS IT ENTERS MY HEAD
THE .38!!!!

. . . AND I HEAR DEATH SAYING HELLO, I'M *HERE!*

O Great Black Masque

O great black masque that is me
that travels with me in spirit
your big eyes that see tomorrows
saw yesterdays and gazes at now
O great black masque of my soul
those ears have heard the clink
of slaves chains and the moans
of sorrow of our past but those
same ears can hear our now
O great black masque that is me
you who copulated with Europe's science
and now dynamically demystifies Europe
O great black masque who is our
ancestors with your cave mouth
filled with sharp teeth to chew
the ropes that bind our hands and our minds
O great black masque you that grins
you that always wins the thrower of
seven cowries and two black eyed dice
O great black masque who says that it
half past pink since white is not a color
O great black masque that carried me from Bouake
to Alabama and back From Mali to Manhattan
O great black masque that dances in me day and night
O black masque of urban guerillas and forest gorillas
O black masque that screams in joy at childbirth and
opens up to the rays of the sun O great black masque
your sharp blade tongue burns war makers buildings
You who stand guard to African breast and soul
O great black masque give us our blacker heavens/
release our minds from borrowed white hells/O great
black masque of Africa O great black masque of all
black people O beautiful black masque Our own black
truth.

CONRAD KENT RIVERS

To Richard Wright

You said that your people
Never knew the full spirit of
Western Civilization.
To be born unnoticed
Is to be born black,
And left out of the grand adventure.

Miseducation, denial,
Are lost in the cruelty of oppression.
And the faint cool kiss of sensuality
Lingers on our cheeks.

The quiet terror brings on silent night.
They are driving us crazy. And our father's
Religion warps his life.

To live day by day
    Is not to live at all.

The Invisible Man

(FOR ELLISON)

Your world is unimportant to me,
I am the man people refuse to see.
My voice is the inner impact of
Everything discontented and lonely.

Your name is meaningless to me,
I am black and white with names.

My soul is a cold grey sheet of
Unrewarded dreams—a satirical design.

I am clustered together like bankers,
Lawyers, judges, doctors, merchants.
I am a bio-chemical accident of epidermis.
A phantom in other people's silly minds.

I am too dark for darkness,
And too black and blue for a shadow.
Because you can see my tears
That makes me disgustingly human.

The Subway

And the subway gives such refinement
To weary souls, and white collars,
Now that the melodic music of typewriters
  is but a thought . . .

Now that the floorwalker, the cigar boss,
The commercial tycoon can be laughed at,
Thought about, cursed out, dehumanized,
  Until nine tomorrow morning . . .

My but the subway is marvelous!
We can dream here, build new worlds.
Let the pregnant stand, let the old folks
Hang on for dear life; we cannot become
Human here, this is our paradise lost.

And like the hum from a drum,
The sub moves on . . .
We must dream quick . . .
Our stop is next . . .

But maybe we should
Ride, ride, ride . . .
To the end of the line.

Prelude

Night and the hood,
soft plain and rape that tears apart.
One man, one child, two human hearts,
destroyed.

Vengeful black hands,
a white body slain. A pause for breath.
One land, one man—then kill again,
a land apart, to dust, to clay.

The Still Voice of Harlem

Come to me broken dreams and all
bring me the glory of fruitless souls,
I shall find a place for them in my gardens.

Weep not for the golden sun of California,
think not of the fertile soil of Alabama . . .
nor your father's eyes, your mother's body twisted
by the washing board.

I am the hope of your unborn,
truly, when there is no more of me . . .
there shall be no more of you . . . .

ETHERIDGE KNIGHT

The Idea of Ancestry

1

Taped to the wall of my cell are 47 pictures: 47 black
faces: my father, mother, grandmothers (1 dead), grand
fathers (both dead), brothers, sisters, uncles, aunts,
cousins (1st & 2nd), nieces, and nephews. They stare
across the space at me sprawling on my bunk. I know
their dark eyes, they know mine. I know their style,
they know mine. I am all of them, they are all of me;
they are farmers, I am a thief, I am me, they are thee.

I have at one time or another been in love with my mother,
1 grandmother, 2 sisters, 2 aunts (1 went to the asylum),
and 5 cousins. I am now in love with a 7 yr old niece
(she sends me letters written in large block print, and
her picture is the only one that smiles at me).

I have the same name as 1 grandfather, 3 cousins, 3 nephews,
and 1 uncle. The uncle disappeared when he was 15, just took
off and caught a freight (they say). He's discussed each year
when the family has a reunion, he causes uneasiness in
the clan, he is an empty space. My father's mother, who is 93
and who keeps the Family Bible with everybody's birth dates
(and death dates) in it, always mentions him. There is no
place in her Bible for "whereabouts unknown."

2

Each Fall the graves of my grandfathers call me, the brown
hills and red gullies of mississippi send out their electric
messages, galvanizing my genes. Last yr/like a salmon quitting
the cold ocean—leaping and bucking up his birthstream/I

hitchhiked my way from L.A. with 16 caps in my pocket and a
monkey on my back. and I almost kicked it with the kinfolks.
I walked barefooted in my grandmother's backyard/I smelled the
old
land and the woods/I sipped cornwhiskey from fruit jars with the
men/
I flirted with the women/I had a ball till the caps ran out
and my habit came down. That night I looked at my grandmother
and split/my guts were screaming for junk/but I was almost
contented/I had almost caught up with me.
(The next day in Memphis I cracked a croaker's crib for a fix.)

This yr there is a gray stone wall damming my stream, and when
the falling leaves stir my genes, I pace my cell or flop on my bunk
and stare at 47 black faces across the space. I am all of them,
they are all of me, I am me, they are thee, and I have no sons
to float in the space between

He Sees Through Stone

He sees through stone
he has the secret
eyes this old black one
who under prison skies
sits pressed by the sun
against the western wall
his pipe between purple gums

the years fall
like overripe plums
bursting red flesh
on the dark earth

his time is not my time
but I have known him
in a time gone

he led me trembling cold
into the dark forest
taught me the secret rites

to take a woman
to be true to my brothers
to make my spear drink
the blood
of my enemies

now black cats circle him
flash white teeth
snarl at the air
mashing green grass beneath
shining muscles
ears peeling his words
he smiles
he knows
the hunt   the enemy
he has the secret eyes
he sees through stone

A Love Poem

I do not expect the spirit of Penelope
To enter my breast, for I am not mighty
Or fearless. (Only our love is brave,
A rock against the wind.) I cry and cringe
When the cyclops peer into my cave.

I do not expect your letters to be lengthy
And of love, flowery and philosophic, for
Words are not our bond.
I need only the hard fact
Of your existence for my subsistence.
Our love is a rock against the wind,
Not soft like silk and lace.

As You Leave Me

Shiny record albums scattered over
the livingroom floor, reflecting light
from the lamp, sharp reflections that hurt

my eyes as I watch you, squatting among the platters,
the beer foam making mustaches on your lips.

And, too,
the shadows on your cheeks from your long lashes
fascinate me—almost as much as the dimples:
in your cheeks, your arms and your legs:
dimples . . . dimples . . . dimples . . .

You
hum along with Mathis—how you love Mathis!
with his burnished hair and quicksilver voice that dances
among the stars and whirls through canyons
like windblown snow. sometimes I think that Mathis
could take you from me if you could be complete
without me. I glance at my watch. it is now time.

You rise,
silently, and to the bedroom and the paint:
on the lips red, on the eyes black,
and I lean in the doorway and smoke, and see you
grow old before my eyes, and smoke. why do you
chatter while you dress, and smile when you grab
your large leather purse? don't you know that when you
leave me I walk to the window and watch you? and light
a reefer as I watch you? and I die as I watch you
disappear in the dark streets
to whistle and to smile at the johns.

Apology for Apostasy?

Soft songs, like birds, die in poison air
So my song cannot now be candy.
Anger rots the oak and elm; roses are rare,
Seldom seen through blind despair.

And my murmur cannot be heard
Above the din and damn. The night is full
Of buggers and bastards; no moon or stars
Light the sky. And my candy is deferred

Till peacetime, when my voice shall be light,
Like down, lilting in the air; then shall I
Sing of beaches, white in the magic sun,
And of moons and maidens at midnight.

For Black Poets Who Think of Suicide

Black Poets should live—not leap
From steel bridges (like the white boys do.
Black Poets should *live*—not lay
Their necks on railroad tracks (like the white boys do.
Black Poets should seek—but not search too much
In sweet dark caves, nor hunt for snipes
Down psychic trails (like the white boys do.

For Black Poets belong to Black People. Are
The Flutes of Black Lovers. Are
The Organs of Black Sorrows. Are
The Trumpets of Black Warriors.
Let all Black Poets die as trumpets,
And be buried in the dust of marching feet.

LeROI JONES

Look for You Yesterday, Here You Come Today

Part of my charm:
envious blues feeling
separation of church & state
grim calls from drunk debutantes

Morning never aids me in my quest.
I have to trim my beard in solitude.
I try to hum lines from "The Poet In New York."

People saw metal all around the house on Saturdays. The Phone
rings.

terrible poems come in the mail. Descriptions of celibate parties
torn trousers: Great Poets dying
with their strophes on. & me
incapable of a simple straight-
forward anger.

It's so diffuse
being alive. Suddenly one is aware
that nobody really gives a damn.
My wife is pregnant with *her* child.
"It means nothing to me," sez Strindberg.

An avalanche of words
could cheer me up. Words from Great Sages.
Was James Karolis a great sage??
Why did I let Ora Matthews beat him up
in the bathroom? Haven't I learned my lesson.

I would take up painting

if I cd think of a way to do it
better than Leonardo. Than Bosch.
Than Hogarth. Than Kline.

Frank walked off the stage, singing
"My silence is as important as Jack's incessant yatter."

I am a mean hungry sorehead.
Do I have the capacity for grace??

To arise one smoking spring
& find one's youth has taken off
for greener parts.

A sudden blankness in the day
as if there were no afternoon.
& all my piddling joys retreated
to their own dopey mythic worlds.

The hours of the atmosphere
grind their teeth like hags.

(When will world war two be over?)

I stood up on a mailbox
waving my yellow tee-shirt
watching the grey tanks
stream up Central Ave.

All these thots
are Flowers Of Evil
cold & lifeless
as subway rails

the sun like a huge cobblestone
flaking its brown slow rays
primititi
once, twice,. My life
seems over & done with.
Each morning I rise
like a sleep walker
& rot a little more.

All the lovely things I've known have disappeared.
I have all my pubic hair & am lonely.
There is probably no such place as BattleCreek, Michigan!

Tom Mix dead in a Boston Nightclub
before I realized what happened.

People laugh when I tell them about Dickie Dare!

What is one to do in an alien planet
where the people breath New Ports?
Where is my space helmet, I sent for it
3 lives ago . . . when there were box tops.

What has happened to box tops??

O, God . . . I must have a belt that glows green
in the dark. Where is my Captain Midnight decoder??
I can't understand what Superman is saying!

THERE MUST BE A LONE RANGER!!!

****

but this also
is part of my charm.
A maudlin nostalgia
that comes on
like terrible thoughts about death.

How dumb to be sentimental about anything
To call it love
& cry pathetically
into the long black handkerchief
of the years.

"Look for you yesterday
Here you come today
Your mouth wide open
But what you got to say?"

—part of my charm

old envious blues feeling
ticking like a big cobblestone clock.

I hear the reel running out . . .
the spectators are impatient for popcorn:
It was only a selected short subject

F. Scott Charon
will soon be glad-handing me
like a legionaire

My silver bullets all gone
My black mask trampled in the dust

& Tonto way off in the hills
moaning like Bessie Smith.

c. 1958

The politics of rich painters

is something like the rest
of our doubt, whatever slow thought
comes to rest, beneath the silence
of starving talk.
Just their fingers' prints
staining the cold glass, is sufficient
for commerce, and a proper ruling on
humanity. You know the pity
of democracy, that we must sit here
and listen to how he made his money.
Tho the catalogue of his possible ignorance
roars and extends through the room
like fire. "Love," becomes the pass,
the word taken intimately to combat
all the uses of language. So that learning
itself falls into disrepute.

2.

What they have gathered into themselves
in that short mean trip from mother's iron tit
to those faggot handmaidens of the french whore

who wades slowly in the narrows, waving her burnt out
torch. There are movies, and we have opinions. There are
regions of compromise so attractive, we daily long
to filthy our minds with their fame. And all the songs
of our handsome generation fall clanging like stones
in the empty darkness of their heads.
                                                  Couples, so beautiful
in the newspapers, marauders of cheap sentiment. So much *taste*
so little understanding, except some up and coming queer explain
cinema and politics while drowning a cigarette.

3.

They are more ignorant than the poor
tho they pride themselves with that accent. And
move easily in fake robes of egalitarianism. Meaning,
I will fuck you even if you don't like art. And are wounded
that you call their italian memories petit bourgeois.
                                                              Whose death
will be Malraux's? Or the names Senghor, Price, Baldwin
whispered across the same dramatic pancakes, to let each eyelash
    flutter
at the news of their horrible deaths. It is a cheap game
to patronize the dead, unless their deaths be accountable
to your own understanding. Which be nothing nothing
if not bank statements and serene trips to our ominous country-
    side.
Nothing, if not whining talk about handsome white men. Nothing
if not false glamourous and static. Except, I admit, your lives
are hideously real.

4.

The source of their art crumbles into legitimate history.
The whimpering pigment of a decadent économy, slashed into
    life
as Yeats' mad girl plummeting over the nut house wall, her broken
knee caps rattling in the weather, reminding us of lands
our antennae do not reach.

And there are people in these savage geographies
use your name in other contexts
think, perhaps, the title of your latest painting
another name for liar.

Poem for HalfWhite College Students

Who are you, listening to me, who are you
listening to yourself? Are you white or
black, or does that have anything to do
with it? Can you pop your fingers to no
music, except those wild monkies go on
in your head, can you jerk, to no melody,
except finger poppers get it together
when you turn from starchecking to checking
yourself. How do you sound, your words, are they
yours? The ghost you see in the mirror, is it really
you, can you swear you are not an imitation greyboy,
can you look right next to you in that chair, and swear,
that the sister you have your hand on is not really
so full of Elizabeth Taylor, Richard Burton is
coming out of her ears. You may even have to be Richard
with a white shirt and face, and four million negroes
think you cute, you may have to be Elizabeth Taylor, old lady,
if you want to sit up in your crazy spot dreaming about dresses,
and the sway of certain porters' hips. Check yourself, learn who it is
speaking, when you make some ultrasophisticated point, check yourself,
when you find yourself gesturing like Steve McQueen, check it out, ask
in your black heart who it is you are, and is that image black or white,

you might be surprised right out the window, whistling dixie on the way in.

c. 1965

A Poem for Black Hearts

For Malcolm's eyes, when they broke
the face of some dumb white man, For
Malcolm's hands raised to bless us
all black and strong in his image
of ourselves, For Malcolm's words
fire darts, the victor's tireless
thrusts, words hung above the world

change as it may, he said it, and
for this he was killed, for saying,
and feeling, and being/change, all
collected hot in his heart, For Malcolm's
heart, raising us above our filthy cities,
for his stride, and his beat, and his address
to the grey monsters of the world, For Malcolm's
pleas for your dignity, black men, for your life,
black man, for the filling of your minds
with righteousness, For all of him dead and
gone and vanished from us, and all of him which
clings to our speech black god of our time.
For all of him, and all of yourself, look up,
black man, quit stuttering and shuffling, look up,
black man, quit whining and stooping, for all of him,
For Great Malcolm a prince of the earth, let nothing in us rest
until we avenge ourselves for his death, stupid animals
that killed him, let us never breath a pure breath if
we fail, and white men call us faggots till the end of
the earth.

Black Art

Poems are bullshit unless they are
teeth or trees or lemons piled
on a step. Or black ladies dying
of men leaving nickel hearts
beating them down. Fuck poems
and they are useful, wd they shoot
come at you, love what you are,
breathe like wrestlers, or shudder
strangely after pissing. We want live
words of the hip world live flesh &
coursing blood. Hearts Brains
Souls splintering fire. We want poems
like fists beating niggers out of Jocks
or dagger poems in the slimy bellies
of the owner-jews. Black poems to
smear on girdlemamma mulatto bitches
whose brains are red jelly stuck
between 'lizabeth taylor's toes. Stinking

Whores! We want "poems that kill."
Assassin poems, Poems that shoot
guns. Poems that wrestle cops into alleys
and take their weapons leaving them dead
with tongues pulled out and sent to Ireland. Knockoff
poems for dope selling wops or slick halfwhite
politicians Airplane poems, rrrrrrrrrrrrrr
rrrrrrrrrrrrrrr . . . tuhtuhtuhtuhtuhtuhtuhtuhtuh
. . . rrrrrrrrrrrrrr . . . Setting fire and death to
whities ass. Look at the Liberal
Spokesman for the jews clutch his throat
& puke himself into eternity . . . rrrrrrr
There's a negroleader pinned to
a bar stool in Sardi's eyeballs melting
in hot flame Another negroleader
on the steps of the white house one
kneeling between the sheriff's thighs
negotiating cooly for his people.
Agggh . . . stumbles across the room . . .
Put it on him, poem. Strip him naked
to the world! Another bad poem cracking
steel knuckles in a jewlady's mouth
Poem scream poison gas on beasts in green berets
Clean out the world for virtue and love,
Let there be no love poems written
until love can exist freely and
cleanly. Let Black People understand
that they are the lovers and the sons
of lovers and warriors and sons
of warriors Are poems & poets &
all the loveliness here in the world

We want a black poem. And a
Black World.
Let the world be a Black Poem
And Let All Black People Speak This Poem
Silently
or LOUD

c. 1965

AUDRE LORDE

Father Son and Holy Ghost

I have not ever seen my father's grave.
Not that his judgment eyes have been forgotten
Nor his great hands print
On our evening doorknobs
One half turn each night and he would come
Misty from the world's business
Massive and silent as the whole day's wish, ready
To re-define each of our shapes—
But that now the evening doorknobs
Wait, and do not recognize us as we pass.

Each week a different woman
Regular as his one quick glass each evening—
Pulls up the grass his stillness grows
Calling it weed. Each week
A different woman has my mother's face
And he, who time has
Changeless
Must be amazed, who knew and loved but one.

My father died in silence, loving creation
And well-defined response.
He lived still judgments on familar things
And died, knowing a January fifteenth that year me.

Lest I go into dust
I have not ever seen my father's grave.

1961

Coal

I
Is the total black, being spoken
From the earth's inside.

There are many kinds of open.
How a diamond comes into a knot of flame
How a sound comes into a word, coloured
By who pays what for speaking.

Some words are open
Like a diamond on glass windows
Singing out within the crash of passing sun
Then there are words like stapled wagers
In a perforated book—buy and sign and tear apart—
And come whatever wills all chances
The stub remains
An ill-pulled tooth with a ragged edge.
Some words live in my throat
Breeding like adders. Others know sun
Seeking like gypsies over my tongue
To explode through my lips
Like young sparrows bursting from shell.
Some words
Bedevil me.

Love is a word another kind of open—
As a diamond comes into a knot of flame
I am black because I come from the earth's inside
Take my word for jewel in your open light.

c. 1964

Naturally

Since Naturally Black is Naturally Beautiful
I must be proud
And, naturally
Black and
Beautiful
Who always was a trifle
Yellow
And plain, though proud,
Before.

Now I've given up pomades
Having spent the summer sunning
And feeling naturally free

(if I die of skin cancer
oh well—one less
black and beautiful me)
Yet no agency spends millions
To prevent my summer tanning
And who trembles nightly
With the fear of their lily cities being swallowed
By a summer ocean of naturally woolly hair?

But I've bought my can of
Natural Hair Spray
Made and marketed in Watts
Still thinking more
Proud beautiful black women
Could better make and use
Black bread.

1968

A Summer Oracle

Without expectation
There is no end
To the shocks of morning
Or even a small summer.

Now the image is fire
Blackening the vague lines
Into defiance across the city.
The image is fire
Sun warming as in a cold country
Barren of symbols for love.

I have forsaken order
And imagine you into fire
Untouchable
In a magician's coat
Covered with signs of destruction and birth
Sewn with griffins and arrows and hammers
And gold sixes stitched into your hem
Your fingers draw fire
But still the old warlocks

Shun you
For no gourds ring in your sack
No spells bring forth
And I am still hungry and fruitless
This summer
The peaches are flinty and juiceless
And cry sour worms.

The image is fire
Flaming over you burning off excess
Like the blaze planters set
To burn off bagasse from their canefields
After a harvest.

The image is fire
The high sign that rules our summer.
I smell it in the charred breezes
Blowing over your body
Close
Hard
Essential
Under its cloak of lies.

1969

A. B. SPELLMAN

Jelly Wrote

jelly wrote,
          you should bc walking on four legs
          but now you're walking on two.
          you know you come directly from the animal famulee

& you do. but dr jive
the winding boy, whose hands only work
was music & pushing
'certain ignorant light skin women' to the corner
was never animal

was never beast in storeyville, refining
a touch for ivory on pool green
with the finest of whorehouse ragtime; use even
for the 'darker niggers music. rough,' jelly wrote
'but they loved it in the tenderloin.'

o the tall & chancey, the ladies'
fancy, the finest boy for miles around,
'your salty dog,' but with diamond incisors,
shooting the agate under a stetson sky
his st louis flats winked into

aaah, mr jelly

1962

John Coltrane

AN IMPARTIAL REVIEW.

may he have new life like the fall
fallen tree, wet moist rotten enough

to see shoots stalks branches & green
leaves (& may the roots) grow into his side.

around the back of the mind, in its closet
is a string, i think, a coil around things
listen to *summertime*, think of spring, negroes
cats in the closet, anything that makes a rock

of your eye. imagine you steal. you are frightened
you want help. you are sorry you are born with ears.

1962

friends i am like you tied

friends i am like you tied
to you & the delicate chain knots
us each to all the moving points
together apart making "the thing"
knotted chain links awkward in knots
knots notted trying to move on impulse
beyond the "us" of us fungus
of the self that eats races whole like you
i am tied
a.b. break something action i've
acted who mans the far end of the i?
that fellow violently inert so placed
so moved from the chair its eye
to filthy window to filthy air to
filthy curb redolent with skid piss
curb street curb skid piss houston st.
moving on down the line you now we
us how stay clean in this place
do not eat soap relevance pays there squats
mundanity kick it in the nuts its crotch swallows
your foot now where are you footless
hiss of the hideous you goofed in the tactic a.b.
you're still too quiet break something larger
who started this war who said there are folk
with culture and good looks let's fry the niggers
in texan shit johnson? kennedy? trumanhoover-
hower?
kid you're ugly ok i told him but don't flatter yourself

you're uglier than that   there is no "this" war
there is no "all" war   either   the west turned
moribund   with marco   the east woke up
with mao   there is war   friends
with sickness and dying   with dying
and hating it   twisting the chain into knots

1965

When Black People Are

when black people are
with each other
we sometimes fear ourselves
whisper over our shoulders
about unmentionable acts
& sometimes we fight & lie.
these are somethings we sometimes do.

& when alone i sometimes walk
from wall to wall fighting visions
of white men fighting me
& black men fighting white men
& fighting me & i lose my
self between walls &
ricocheting shots & can't say
for certain who i have killed
or been killed by.

it is the fear of winter passing
& summer coming & the killing
i have called for coming
to my door saying
hit it a.b., you're in it too.

& the white army moves like thieves
in the night mass producing beautiful
black corpses & then stealing them away
while my frequent death watches me
from orangeburg on cronkite &
i'm oiling my gun & cooking my food
& saying "when the time comes"
to myself, over & over, hopefully.

but i remember driving from atlanta
to the city with stone & featherstone
& cleve & on the way feather talked
about ambushing a pair of klansmen
& cleve told how they hunted
cheney's body in the white night
of the haunted house in the mississippi
swamp while a runaway survivor
from orangeburg slept between wars
on the back seat.
times like this
are times when black people
are with each other & the strength flows
back & forth between us like
borrowed breath.

1968

BOB KAUFMAN

I Have Folded My Sorrows

I have folded my sorrows into the mantle of summer night,
Assigning each brief storm its allotted space in time,
Quietly pursuing catastrophic histories buried in my eyes.
And yes, the world is not some unplayed Cosmic Game,
And the sun is still ninety-three million miles from me,
And in the imaginary forest, the shingled hippo becomes the gay
unicorn.
No, my traffic is not with addled keepers of yesterday's disasters,
Seekers of manifest disembowelment on shafts of yesterday's pains.
Blues come dressed like introspective echoes of a journey.
And yes, I have searched the rooms of the moon on cold summer
nights.
And yes, I have refought those unfinished encounters.
Still, they remain unfinished.
And yes, I have at times wished myself something different.

The tragedies are sung nightly at the funerals of the poet;
The revisited soul is wrapped in the aura of familiarity.

African Dream

In black core of night, it explodes
Silver thunder, rolling back my brain,
Bursting copper screens, memory worlds
Deep in star-fed beds of time,
Seducing my soul to diamond fires of night.
Faint outline, a ship—momentary fright
Lifted on waves of color,
Sunk in pits of light,
Drummed back through time,
Hummed back through mind,

Drumming, cracking the night.
Strange forest songs, skin sounds
Crashing through—no longer strange.
Incestuous yellow flowers tearing
Magic from the earth.
Moon-dipped rituals, led
By a scarlet god,
Caressed by ebony maidens
With daylight eyes,
Purple garments,
Noses that twitch,
Singing young girl songs
Of an ancient love
In dark, sunless places
Where memories are sealed,
Burned in eyes of tigers.

Suddenly wise, I fight the dream:
Green screams enfold my night.

Walking Parker Home

Sweet beats of jazz impaled on slivers of wind
Kansas Black Morning/First Horn Eyes/
Historical sound pictures on New Bird wings
People shouts/boy alto dreams/Tomorrow's
Gold belled pipe of stops and future Blues Times
Lurking Hawkins/shadows of Lester/realization
Bronze fingers—brain extensions seeking trapped sounds
Ghetto thoughts/bandstand courage/solo flight
Nerve-wracked suspicions of newer songs and doubts
New York altar city/black tears/secret disciples
Hammer horn pounding soul marks on unswinging gates
Culture gods/mob sounds/vision of spikes
Panic excursions to tribal Jazz wombs and transfusions
Heroin nights of birth/and soaring/over boppy new ground.
Smothered rage covering pyramids of notes spontaneously exploding
Cool revelations/shrill hopes/beauty speared into greedy ears
Birdland nights on bop mountains, windy saxophone revolutions
Dayrooms of junk/and melting walls and circling vultures/
Money cancer/remembered pain/terror flights/
Death and indestructible existence

In that Jazz corner of life
Wrapped in a mist of sound
His legacy, our Jazz-tinted dawn
Wailing his triumphs of oddly begotten dreams
Inviting the nerveless to feel once more
That fierce dying of humans consumed
In raging fires of Love.

Blues Note

Ray Charles is the black wind of Kilimanjaro,
Screaming up-and-down blues,
Moaning happy on all the elevators of my time.

Smiling into the camera, with an African symphony
Hidden in his throat, and *(I Got a Woman)* wails, too.

He burst from Bessie's crushed black skull
One cold night outside of Nashville, shouting,
And grows bluer from memory, glowing bluer, still.

At certain times you can see the moon
Balanced on his head.

From his mouth he hurls chunks of raw soul.
He separated the sea of polluted sounds
And led the blues into the Promised Land.

Ray Charles is a dangerous man ('way cross town),
And I love him.

for Ray Charles's birthday
N.Y.C./1961

Mingus

String-chewing bass players,
Plucking rolled balls of sound
From the jazz-scented night.

Feeding hungry beat seekers
Finger-shaped heartbeats,
Driving ivory nails
Into their greedy eyes.

Smoke crystals, from the nostrils
Of released jazz demons,
Crash from foggy yesterday
To the light
Of imaginary night.

High on Life

Floating on superficially elevated streets
secretly nude,
Subtle forked tongues of sensuous fog
probe and core
Deliciously into my chapped-lipped pores
coolly whistling,
Spiraling in hollowed caves of skin-stretched me,
totally doorless,
Emptied of vital parts, previously evicted finally
by landlord mind
To make nerve-lined living space, needed desperately
by my transient, sightless, sleepless,
Soul.

Benediction

Pale brown Moses went down to Egypt land
To let somebody's people go.
Keep him out of Florida, no UN there:
The poor governor is all alone,
With six hundred thousand illiterates.

America, I forgive you . . . I forgive you
Nailing black Jesus to an imported cross
Every six weeks in Dawson, Georgia.
America, I forgive you . . . I forgive you
Eating black children, I know your hunger.
America, I forgive you . . . I forgive you

Burning Japanese babies defensively—
I realize how necessary it was.
Your ancestor had beautiful thoughts in his brain.
His descendants are experts in real estate.
Your generals have mushrooming visions.
Every day your people get more and more
Cars, televisions, sickness, death dreams.
You must have been great
Alive.

SONIA SANCHEZ

malcolm

do not speak to me of martyrdom
of men who die to be remembered
on some parish day.
i don't believe in dying
though i too shall die
and violets like castanets
will echo me.

yet this man
this dreamer,
thick-lipped with words
will never speak again
and in each winter
when the cold air cracks
with frost, i'll breathe
his breath and mourn
my gun-filled nights.
he was the sun that tagged
the western sky and
melted tiger-scholars
while they searched for stripes.
he said, "fuck you white
man. we have been
curled too long. nothing
is sacred now. not your
white faces nor any
land that separates
until some voices
squat with spasms."

do not speak to me of living.
life is obscene with crowds
of white on black.
death is my pulse.
what might have been

is not for him/or me
but what could have been
floods the womb until i drown.

1966

from right on: wite america

this country might have
been a pio
          neer land
once.
     but.   there ain't
no mo
      indians   blowing
custer's mind
             with a different
image of america.
                  this country
might have
          needed shoot/
outs/daily/
          once.
               but there ain't
no mo real/wite/   all american
                     bad/guys.
just.
    u & me.
           blk/and un/armed.
this country might have
been a pion
          eer land.   once.
                             and it still is.
check out
         the falling
gun/shells   on our blk/tomorrows.

1968

liberation/poem

blues ain't culture
                  they sounds of
oppression

against the white man's
shit/
game he's run on us all
these blue/yrs.
blues is struggle
strangulation
of our people
cuz we cudn't off the
white motha/fucka
soc/king it to us
but. now.
when i hear billie's soft
soul/ful/sighs
of "am i blue"
i say
no. sweet/billie.
no mo.
no mo
blue/trains running on this track
they all been de/railed.
am i blue?
sweet/baby/blue/
billie.
no. i'm blk/
& ready.

1968

last poem i'm gonna write about us

some
times i dream bout
u & me
runnen down
a street laughen.
me no older
u no younger
than we be.
& we finalee catch
each other.
laugh. tooouch
in the nite.

some
times
i turn a corner
of my mind
& u be there
loooooking
at me.
& smilen.
yo/far/away/smile.
& i moooove
to u.
& the day is not any day. & yes ter day
is looonNNg
goooNNe. & we just be. Some
times i be steady dreamen bout u
cuz i waaannNt
neeeeEEeeD u so
baaaaAdDD.
with u no younger &
me no older
than we be.

1969

blk/rhetoric

(FOR KILEBREW KEEBY, ICEWATER
BAKER, GARY ADAMS AND OMAR SHABAZZ)

who's gonna make all
that beautiful blk/rhetoric
mean something.
like
i mean
who's gonna take
the words
blk/is/beautiful
and make more of it
than blk/capitalism.
u dig?
i mean
like who's gonna

take all the young/long/haired
natural/brothers and sisters
and let them
grow till
all that is
impt is them
selves
moving in straight/
revolutionary/lines
toward the enemy
(and we know who that is)
like. man.
who's gonna give our young
blk/people new heroes
(instead of catch/phrases)
(instead of cad/ill/acs)
(instead of pimps)
(instead of wite/whores)
(instead of drugs)
(instead of new dances)
(instead of chit/ter/lings)
(instead of a 35¢ bottle of ripple)
(instead of quick/fucks in the hall/way
of wite/america's mind)
like. this. is an S O S
me. calling . . . .
calling . . . .
some / one
pleasereplysoon.

1969

LUCILLE CLIFTON

In the Inner City

in the inner city
or
like we call it
home
we think a lot about uptown
and the silent nights
and the houses straight as
dead men
and the pastel lights
and we hang on to our no place
happy to be alive
and in the inner city
or
like we call it
home

1967

My Mamma Moved Among the Days

My Mama moved among the days
like a dreamwalker in a field;
seemed like what she touched was hers
seemed like what touched her couldn't hold,
she got us almost through the high grass
then seemed like she turned around and ran
right back in
right back on in

1967

Miss Rosie

When I watch you
wrapped up like garbage

sitting, surrounded by the smell
of too old potato peels
or
when I watch you
in your old man's shoes
with the little toe cut out
sitting, waiting for your mind
like next week's grocery
I say
when I watch you
you wet brown bag of woman
who used to be the best looking gal in Georgia
used to be called the Georgia Rose
I stand up
through your destruction
I stand up

1967

Good Times

My Daddy has paid the rent
and the insurance man is gone
and the lights is back on
and my uncle Brud has hit
for one dollar straight
and they is good times
good times
good times

My Mamma has made bread
and Grampaw has come
and everybody is drunk
and dancing in the kitchen
and singing in the kitchen
oh these is good times
good times
good times

oh children think about the
good times

1967

Ca'line's Prayer

I have got old
in a desert country
I am dry
and black as drought
don't make water
only acid
even dogs don't drink

Remember me from Wydah
Remember the child
running across Dahomey
black as ripe papaya
juicy as sweet berries
and set me in the rivers of your glory

Ye Ma Jah

1968

the lost baby poem

the time i dropped your almost body down
down to meet the waters under the city
and run one with the sewage to the sea
what did i know about waters rushing back
what did i know about drowning
or being drowned

you would have been born into winter
in the year of the disconnected gas
and no car   we would have made the thin
walk over Genesee hill into the Canada wind
to watch you slip like ice into strangers' hands
you would have fallen naked as snow into winter
if you were here i could tell you these
and some other things

if i am ever less than a mountain
for your definite brothers and sisters
let the rivers pour over my head
let the sea take me for a spiller
of seas   let black men call me stranger
always for your never named sake.

let the sea take me for a spiller
of seas   let black men call me stranger
always   for your never named sake

1969

after kent state

only to keep
his little fear
he kills his cities
and his trees
even his children   oh
people
white ways are
the way of death
come into the
Black
and live

1970

CLARENCE MAJOR

Celebrated Return

1. a circus of battleships carrying heavy laughter passes
beneath a bridge which may be lifted and each ship
has a drift. thus they move.
they had just left the land where dromedaries are plenty
and men go in droll groups in robes. they wear beards
and keep their women subdued. and their laughter remains
an excavated kind of shelter for the dubious plight of anger.

2. ashore gawky measures of simple people wait for their
arrival. not ever dreaming of what pushes their lives nor
the waves back and forth. as the ships circle the geometry
of the solid sunstruck shouts. now at last.
their christian celebration.

GLORIA IN EXCELSIS
GLORIA IN EXCELSIS
GLORIA IN EXCELSIS
GLORIA PATRI
GLORIA PATRI
GLORIA PATRI

Flesh Line, the Space

there is a girl
i used to go with, that is
perform do enter uprear charm
she could in 5 min
i married her
we yapped money & problems, she couldn't
anymore. Politics

movement between our lines, our legal

thing. I (used) lie beside her
eyes up
flight of dark wings caught in a narrow dusty
stair–
way, breaking, things that desperate. My health
you know.
And talk, lines hung weapons between
us. Like I see her now
but keep thinking of
her as dead.

1965

Dismal Moment, Passing

this is has to be here
because I am dis-
consolated.

Even summer coming
4 years ago, now enlarges the green
accuracy of nature,
which we won't see till Mexico, any-
way. I think of my mother when I think
of nature, her beliefs. Those lies in space
hanging there to arrange
human minds like suffixes to structures,
like societies. Or meaning like a sheet flapping
on a back porch, people might still
wash things, hang them up to dry. Like children
playing roots or shock on the side—
where we walk, upsidedown looking at jets go

not easy like me here, in this opaque opening.
And promise to be All Right
tomorrow, yes yes

1966

Longlegs

her Cool was a
northern thing
brought from the south

she really stretched out in NYC

long-
legs now step
silently in narrow streets
in the village

sleep on easy floors
dark travels on
high tongue eye trips
or the indispensable

devotion to music she
works for her Cool
she really stretched out for real

in protective winter
nights her yoga and

diluted footfalls thru
parks of drums, night

challenge the tender pot
reek LSD, even beyond acid

to hieroglyphics on the
flesh of her reference

figures that rigid-
situations put pressure

thru after all europe
mexico west coast & NYC

could even define, or should
necessarily she just

is a rapid position-girl
change case memory

of self efficient calm
in her private rites

1967

KEORAPETSE KGOSITSILE

Brother Malcolm's Echo

Translated furies ring
on the page not thoughts
about life
but what should be
real people and things
loving love
this is real
the human Spirit moves
what should be
grinning molotov cocktails
replenishing the fire
WATTS happening
SHARPEVILLE burning
much too damn talking
is not
what's happening

Mandela's Sermon

Blessed are the dehumanized
For they have nothing to lose
But their patience.

False gods killed the poet in me. Now
I dig graves
With artistic precision.

Song for Aimé Césaire

The fragrance of rebirth
is the rhythm of our movement

as I laugh
or jumpandlaugh
on time or stone
but I cannot lean on the groaning years
breathing on time
as wave rides on wave
as Detroit follows Newark
Setif Sharpeville
We revere you, Césaire
for now we know
icebergs can go up in flames
we know
we cannot lean on time
because in every corner of the memory
the years are groaning
for us to up and blaze
so I jump or laugh on time or stone
as my heads spits flames
from Zimbabwe to Watts recreating
elegant memories of you.

The Elegance of Memory

Distances separate bodies not people. Ask
Those who have known sadness or joy
The bone of feeling is pried open
By a song, the elegance
Of color, a familiar smell, this
Flower or the approach of an evening . . .

All this is NOW

I used to wonder
Was her grave warm enough,
'Madikeledi, my grandmother,
As big-spirited as she was big-legged,
She would talk to me. She would . . .
How could I know her sadness then
Or who broke my father's back?
But now . . .

The elegance of memory,

Deeper than the grave
Where she went before I could
Know her sadness, is larger
Than the distance between
My country and I. Things more solid
Than the rocks with which those sinister
Thieves tried to break our back.

I hear her now. And I wonder
Now does she know the strength of the fabric
She wove in my heart for us? . . . Her
Voice clearer now than then: 'Boykie,
Don't ever take any nonsense from *them*,
You hear!'

There are memories between us
Deeper than grief. There are
Feelings between us much stronger
Than the cold enemy machine that breaks
The back. Sister, there are places between us
Deeper than the ocean, no distances.
Pry your heart open, Brother, mine too,
Learn to love the clear voice
The music in the memory pried
Open to the bone of feeling, no distances

JULIA FIELDS

I Heard a Young Man Saying

I heard a young man saying
In the green afternoon,
In the sun-swept afternoon,
In the bees drone afternoon,
In the peaceful, splendid afternoon,

—War—
There's talk of war
Another decade. Another war.
One grown-up generation toward war.
Somehow, I planned on living.
What was the matter with me?
War. There's talk of war.'

I, a woman, listened by the door,
By the broken-hinged door,
'I somehow planned on living.'

Something plans these things.
The echo of the innocent words
Squirmed after me down the stairs,
Something plans these things . . .

1958

No Time for Poetry

Midnight is no time for
Poetry—
  The heart is much too
calm
  The spirit too lagging
  and dull—
But the morning!

With the sunshine in one's eyes
and breath—
And all the pink clouds
Like chiffon in a dressing gown
And the orange-white mists
That leap and furl—

Ah, I should greet the morning
  As though I never saw a morning before
And only heard that it
  was this or that,
Gossip that was good either way,
There being nothing derogatory to say.

And in that strange-white mist
I'd be content to go upon the paths
with neither shoes nor hat
winding my way away from home
much like a
  cornerless cat
Holding vibrations of laughter in my
Fur
  That floated from who knows where
  and goes who-less-could-care.

There are no orange-white mists
  at midnight
  They are a world away
  And so
  Midnight is not time for Poetry

1958

Madness One Monday Evening

Late that mad Monday evening
I made mermaids come from the sea
As the block sky sat
Upon the waves
And night came
Creeping up to me

(I tell you I made mermaids
Come from the sea)

The green waves lulled and rolled
As I sat by the locust tree
And the bright glare of the neon world
Sent gas-words bursting free—
Their spued splendour fell on the billows
And gustily it grew to me
As I sat up upon the shore
And made mermaids come from the sea.

1959

Poem

Let us poets put away our pens
If all we must write are
Eulogies—
If all we must write are
Tears
For our dead heroes
If we must ever despair
And never rejoice.

Our blood dries upon the pages
Our black ink dries
In time with their black blood.
And is this what we—
The "intellectuals"—
Offer as our share to the ages?
Is this our gift?

Will time be cognizant
That we
In our little rooms
Bent our heads
And scribbled there
As the red blood from
Dying men dribbled everywhere?

The poets' blood is rushing
Rushing onto white leaves

Of paper—
Rushing, the poet's thoughts
Rushing onto white sheafs
Of paper
On the battle fields of
Sacrifice
Our heroes are perishing
One by one
Early to their graves they go.
One by one.
Our heroes martyred
One by one.
Count the number gone.
I live, you live.
How are we remiss? Is death not the style?
The best are dying.
The cowardly must mourn.
One by one.
Count the heroes gone
Early to their graves.
The best are dying.

At the start of the cold year,
Malcolm left us.
Hunted, shattered by a gun.
That was one.
He lay upon the ground
While the people
Ringed him round
With their terror and their fear.
His lips grasped at air
His heart froze
And all his intelligent stare
Was one frigid gaze
Into the snow blanked sky.
That was a mighty one.
And even then the blood
Of Mack and Medgar
Was drying in the earth.
And that was three.
Now Martin. The Benevolent.
That was one
Mack, Medgar, Malcolm, Martin.

Is Mercy also dead?
And Malice? Is Malice dead?
And is that six?

When I heard
I could not weep
So dry my eyes
So dry my heart.
One dangerous dreamer gone.
Another one.
And all to be heard
Were the voices, voices, voices.
The clever talking death to death.
In the spring of the year.
And the dumb birds
Singing, Singing, Singing
"Let the dead bury the dead"
And the poets writing.
In their little rooms,
The poets bent
Over sheets of paper
And their pens
Moving—line by line
Their little eulogies
Eloquent, impotent
Polished, meaningless
One by one

In this Maw of the world
The dead are burying the dead.
Hatred the Pallbearer is
Bearing all away.
Hatred the Pallbearer leads
The Honor Guard, is
Bearing all away.

And will the people
Sit in their houses,
Gaze from their window
And their doors forever,
And will they mourn
Forever from the rooftops
And the trees?

And will they always Kill the Dreamer?
One by One.
And the voices start.
Mourning death to death.
The celebration by
The ceremonial tongues of Power
Talking death to death.
And the contrite pens
Writing and writing all. Writing death to death
And everywhere the hearts
Seal up the books
And sing and write no more.

1968

High on the Hog

Take my share of Soul Food—
I do not wish
To taste of pig
    Of either gut
        Or grunt
        From bowel
            Or jowl

I want caviar
Shrimp soufflé
Sherry
  Champagne
        And not because
    These are the
    Whites' domain
    But just because
    I'm entitled—

For I've been
        V.d.'d enough
        T.b.'d enough
    and
  Hoe-cake fed Knock-Knee'd enough
  Spindly led-bloodhound tree'd enough
        To eat
        High on the Hog

I've been
Hired last
Fired first enough
I've sugar-watered my
Thirst enough—

Been lynched enough
Slaved enough
Cried enough
Died enough

Been deprived—
Have survived enough
To eat
High on the Hog.
Keep the black-eyed peas
And the grits,
The high blood-pressure chops
And gravy sops

I want apertifs supreme
Baked Alaska—
Something suave, cool
For I've been considered faithful fool
From 40 acres and a mule . . .

I've been
Slighted enough
Sever-righted enough
And up tighted enough
And I want
High on the Hog

For dragging the cotton sack
On bended knees
In burning sun
In homage to the
Great King cotton
For priming the money-green tobacco
And earning pocket-change

For washing in iron pots
For warming by coal and soot

For eating the leavings from
Others' tables

I've lived my wretched life
Between domestic rats
And foreign wars
Carted to my final rest
In second-hand cars

But I've been leeched enough
Dixie-peached enough
Color bleached enough

And I want
High on the Hog!

Oh, I've heard the Mau Maus
Screaming

Romanticising Pain
I hear them think
They go against the Grain

But I've lived in shacks
Long enough
Had strong black beaten
Backs long enough

And I've been
Urban-planned
Been Monyihanned
Enough
And I want
High on the Hog

1969

DON L. LEE

The negro

(A PURE PRODUCT OF AMERICANISM)

Swinging, Swinging,
thru cotton fields,
small southern towns,
big ghetto darkness where
his mind was blown,
Swinging, Swinging,
to assimilation into whi
te madness called civilization/
by those who have the
power to define,
Swinging, Swinging,
with power to define, whi
te power; indians were never
the victors—they massacred/
black history was booker t.
& george c. & a whi-te lie
over black truth,
Swinging, Swinging,
with ray charles singing
the stars sprangle banner/
all his soul didn't change the
colors/red, white & light blue,
Swinging, Swinging,
working, saving all year/
working, saving to buy
christmas gifts for children/
just to tell them a whi
te santa claus brought them,
Swinging, Swinging,
into aberration where there
is a black light trying to

penetrate that whi-teness
called mr. clean,
Swinging, Swinging,
into blackness/away from
negroness/to Self to
awareness of basic color/
my color, i found it,
Swinging, Swinging,
by
his
neck. (nigger)

a poem to complement other poems

change.
life if u were a match i wd light u into something beautiful. change.
change.
for the better into a realreal together thing. change, from a make believe
nothing on corn meal and water. change.
change. from the last drop to the first, maxwellhouse did. change.
change was a programmer for IBM, thought him was a brown computor. change.
colored is something written on southern outhouses. change.
grayhound did, i mean they got rest rooms on buses. change.
change.
change nigger.
saw a nigger hippy, him wanted to be different. changed.
saw a nigger liberal, him wanted to be different. changed.
saw a nigger conservative, him wanted to be different. changed.
niggers don't u know that niggers are different. change.
a doublechange. nigger wanted a double zero in front of his name; a license to kill,
niggers are licensed to be killed. change. a negro: something pigs eat.

change. i say change into a realblack righteous aim. like
i don't play
saxophone but that doesn't mean i don't dig 'trane.'
change.
change.
hear u coming but yr/steps are too loud. change. even a
lamp post changes nigger.
change, stop being an instant yes machine. change.
niggers don't change they just grow. that's a change;
bigger & better niggers.
change, into a necessary blackself.
change, like a gas meter gets higher.
change, like a blues song talking about a righteous tomorrow.
change, like a tax bill getting higher.
change, like a good sister getting better.
change, like knowing wood will burn. change.
know the realenemy.
change,
change nigger: standing on the corner, thought him was
cool. him still
standing there. it's winter time, him cool.
change,
know the realenemy.
change: him wanted to be a TV star. him is. ten o'clock
news.
wanted, wanted. nigger stole some lemon & lime
popsicles,
thought them were diamonds.
change nigger change.
know the realenemy.
change: is u is or is u aint. change. now now change. for
the better change.
read a change. live a change. read a blackpoem.
change. be the realpeople.
change. blackpoems
will change:
know the realenemy. change. know the realenemy. change
yr/enemy change know the real
change know the realenemy change, change, know the
realenemy, the realenemy, the real
realenemy change your the enemies/change your change
your change your enemy change

your enemy. know the realenemy, the world's enemy.
    know them know them know them the
realenemy change your enemy change your change
    change change your enemy change change
change change your change change change
your
mind nigger.

But He Was Cool
or: he even stopped for green lights

super-cool
ultrablack
a tan/purple
had a beautiful shade.

he had a double-natural
that wd put the sisters to shame.
his dashikis were tailor made
& his beads were imported sea shells
    (from some blk/country i never heard of)
he was triple-hip.

his tikis were hand carved
out of ivory
& came express from the motherland.
he would greet u in swahili
& say good-by in yoruba.
woooooooooooo-jim he bes so cool & ill tel li gent
        cool-cool is so cool he was un-cooled by
            other niggers' cool
        cool-cool ultracool was bop-cool/ice box
            cool so cool cold cool
        his wine didn't have to be cooled, he was
            air conditioned cool
        cool-cool/real cool made me cool—now
            ain't that cool
        cool-cool so cool him nick-named refrig-
            erator.

cool-cool so cool

he didn't know,
after detroit, newark, chicago &c.,
we had to hip
                    cool-cool/super-cool/real cool
               that
to be black
is
to be
very-hot.

Blackman/an unfinished history

the old musician   beat into an alien image of nothingness
we
remember you & will not forget
the days, the nights, the weekends
the secret savings for the trip north
or up south. We entered the new cities—
they were not ready for us—
those on the great rivers, the lakes
they were clean then, somewhat pure,
u cd even drink fr/them
& the fish lived there in abundance.
We came by backseat greyhound & special trains
up south came us
to become a part of the pot that was supposed to melt
                    it did and we burned
and we burned into something different & unknown
we acquired a new ethic   a new morality   a new history
and we lost
we lost much   we lost that   that was
we became americans   the best   the real
and blindly adopted america's heroes as our own
our minds wouldn't *function*
what was wrong?
it couldn't have been the air   it was clean then.

today
from the clouds we look back
seat 16C in the bird with the golden wings.
we came & were different shades of darkness

& we brought our music and dance,
that which wasn't polluted.
we took on the language, manners, mores, dress & religion
of the people with the unusual color.
into the 20th century we wandered rubber-stamped
a poor copy!

but the music was ours, the dance was ours, was ours.
& then it was hip—it was hip
to walk, talk & act a certain neighborhoodway,
we wore 24 hr sunglasses & called our woman *baby,*
our woman,
we wished her something else,
& she became that wish.
she developed into what we wanted,
she not only reflected *her,* but reflected us,
was a mirror of our death-desires.
we failed to protect or respect her
& no one else would,
& we didn't understand, we didn't understand.
why,
she be doing the things she don't do.

the sixties brought us black
at different levels, at different colors we searched
while some of us still pissed into the wind.
we tasted
& turned our heads into a greater vision.
greatness becomes our new values—OOOOOOOO
like telling yr daughter she's beautiful
& meaning *it.* Vee. Boom Veeeee Boom
You going to do it jim! BOOOOOOOOM
You goin ta jump around & startle the world blackman.
goin ta space man, all u got ta do is think space thoughts.
You're *slick* jim, yes you is
slicker than a oil slick, yes you is
just been sliding in the wrong direction. click.
be a *New World* picture. click, click.
blackman click blackman click into tomorrow.
Spaced from the old thoughts into
the new. Zooomm. Zoooommmmm Zooommmmmm.
click

design yr own neighborhoods, Zoom it can be,
teach yr own children, Zoom Zoom it can be,
build yr own loop, Zoom Zoom it can be,
feed yr own people. Zoom Zoom it can be,
Watch out world greatness is coming. click click.
protect yr own communities, Zoom Zoom it can be.

create *man* blackman . . . .
walk thru the
world
as if You are world itself, click.
be an extension of everything beautiful & powerful, click
click.
HEY blackman look like
you'd be named something
like . . . . *earth, sun*
or *mountain.*
Go head, *universe*
Zoommmmmmmm Zooommmmmmmmmm
Zooooommmmmmmmmmmmm click click.
be it,
blackman.

Change is Not Always Progress

(FOR AFRICA & AFRICANS)

Africa.

don't let them
steal
your face or
take your circles
and make them squares.

don't let them
steel
your body as to put
100 stories of concrete on you

so that you
arrogantly
scrape
the
sky.

We Walk the Way of the New World

1.

we run the dangercourse.
the way of the stocking caps & murray's grease.
(if u is modern u used duke greaseless hair pomade)
jo jo was modern/an international nigger
born: jan. 1, 1863 in new york, mississippi
his momma was mo militant than he was/is
jo jo bes no instant negro
his development took all of 106 years
& he was the first to be stamped "made in USA"
where he arrived bow-legged a curve ahead of the 20th
century's new weapon: television.
which invented, "how to win and influence people"
& gave jo jo his how/ever look: however u want me.

we discovered that with the right brand of cigarettes
that one, with his best girl,
cd skip thru grassy fields in living color
& in slow-motion: Caution: niggers, cigarette smoking
will kill u & yr/health.
& that the breakfast of champions is: blackeyed peas & rice.
& that God is dead & Jesus is black and last seen on 63rd
street in a gold & black dashiki, sitting in a pink
hog speaking swahili with a pig-latin accent.
& that integration and coalition are synonymous,
& that the only thing that really mattered was:
who could get the highest on the least or how to expand
& break one's mind.

in the coming world
new prizes are

to be given
we *ran* the dangercourse.
now, it's a silent walk/a careful eye
jo jo is there
to his mother he is unknown
(she accepted with a newlook: what wd u do if someone
loved u?)
jo jo is back
& he will catch all the new jo jo's as they wander in & out
and with a fan-like whisper say: you ain't no
tourist
and Harlem ain't for
sight-seeing, brother.

2.

Start with the itch and there will be no scratch. Study
yourself.
Watch yr/every movement as u skip thru-out the southside of
chicago.
be hip to yr/actions.

our dreams are realities
traveling the nature-way.
we meet them
at the apex of their utmost
meanings/means;
we walk in cleanliness
down state st/or Fifth Ave.
& wicked apartment buildings shake
as their windows announce our presence
as we jump into the interior
& cut the day's evil away.
We walk in cleanliness
the newness of it all
becomes us
our women listen to us
and learn.
We teach our children thru
our actions.

We'll become owners of the New World

the New World.
will run it as unowners
for
we will live in it too
& will want to be remembered
as   realpeople.

Move Un-noticed to be Noticed: A Nationhood Poem

move, into our own, not theirs
into our.
they own it (for the moment): the unclean world, the
                    polluted space, the un-censor-
                    ed air, yr/foot steps as they
                    run wildly in the wrong
                    direction.
move, into our own, not theirs
into our.
move, you can't buy own.
own is like yr/hair (if u let it live); a natural extension of
    ownself.
own is yr/reflection, yr/total-being; the way u walk, talk,
        dress and relate to each other is *own.*
own is you,
cannot be bought or sold: can u buy yr/writing hand
                    yr/dancing feet, yr/speech,
                    yr/woman (if she's real),
                    yr/manhood?
own is ours.
all we have to do is   *take it,*
take it the way u take from one another,
        the way u take artur rubenstein over thelonious
            monk,
        the way u take eugene genovese over lerone bennett,
        the way u take robert bly over imamu baraka,
        the way u take picasso over charles white,
        the way u take marianne moore over gwendolyn
            brooks,
        the way u take *inaction* over *action.*

move. move to act.   act.
act into thinking and think into action.
try to think. think.   try to think think think.
try to think. think (like i said, into yr/own) think.
try to think. don't hurt yourself, i know it's new.
try to act,
act into thinking and think into action.
can u do it, hunh? i say hunh, can you stop moving like a drunk
    gorilla?
                    ha ha   che che
                    ha ha   che che
                    ha ha   che che
                    ha ha   che che
move
what is u anyhow: a professional car watcher, a billboard for
    nothingness, a sane madman, a reincarnated clark gable?
either you is or you ain't!

the deadliving
are the worldmakers,
the image breakers,
the rule takers: blackman can you stop a hurricane?

"I remember back in 1954 or '55, in Chicago, when we had
13 days without a murder, that was before them colored
people started calling themselves *black*."
move.
move,
move to be moved,
move into yr/ownself, Clean.
Clean, u is the first black hippy i've ever met.
why u bes dressen so funny, anyhow, hunh?
i mean, is that u Clean?
why u bes dressen like an airplane, can u fly,

i mean,
will yr/blue jim-shoes fly u,
& what about yr/tailor made bell bottoms, Clean?
can they lift u above madness,
turn u into the right direction,
& that red & pink scarf around yr/neck what's that for Clean,
hunh?   will it help u fly, yeah, swing, swing   ing swing
        swinging high above telephone wires with dreams

of this & that and illusions of trying to take bar-b-q
ice cream away from lion minded niggers who
didn't even know that *polish* is more than a
sausage.
"clean as a tack,
rusty as a nail,
haven't had a bath
sence columbus sail."

when u goin be something real, Clean?
like yr/own, yeah, when u goin be yr/ownself?

the deadliving
are the worldmakers,
the image breakers,
the rule takers: blackman can u stop a hurricane, mississippi
couldn't.
blackman if u can't stop what mississippi couldn't, *be it. be it.*
blackman be the wind, be the win, the win, the win, win win:

wooooooooooowe boom boom wooooooooooowe bah
wooooooooooowe boom boom wooooooooooowe bah
if u can't stop a hurricane, be one.
wooooooooooowe boom boom wooooooooooowe bah
wooooooooooowe boom boom wooooooooooowe bah
be the baddddest hurricane that ever came, a black hurricane.
wooooooooooowe boom boom wooooooooooowe bah
wooooooooooowe boom boom wooooooooooowe bah
the badddest black hurricane that ever came, a black
hurricane named Beulah,
go head Beulah, do the hurricane.
wooooooooooowe boom boom wooooooooooowe bah
wooooooooooowe boom boom wooooooooooowe bah
move
move to be moved from the un-moveable,
into our own, yr/self is own, yrself is own, own yourself.
go where you/we go, hear the unheard and do,
do the undone, do it, do it, do it *now,* Clean
and tomorrow your sons will
be alive to praise
you.

NIKKI GIOVANNI

Nikki-Rosa

childhood remembrances are always a drag
if you're Black
you always remember things like living in Woodlawn
with no inside toilet
and if you become famous or something
they never talk about how happy you were to have your mother
all to your self and
how good the water felt when you got your bath from one of those
big tubs that folk in chicago barbecue in
and somehow when you talk about home
it never gets across how much you
understood their feelings
as the whole family attended meetings about Hollydale
and even though you remember
your biographers never understand
your father's pain as he sells his stock
and another dream goes
and though you're poor it isn't poverty that
concerns you
and though they fought a lot
it isn't your father's drinking that makes any difference
but only that everybody is together and you
and your sister have happy birthdays and very good christmasses
and I really hope no white person ever has cause to write about me
because they never understand Black love is Black wealth and they'll
probably talk about my hard childhood and never understand that
all the while I was quite happy.

1968

Adulthood

(FOR CLAUDIA)

i usta wonder who i'd be
when i was a little girl in indianapolis

sitting on doctors porches with post-dawn pre-debs
(wondering would my aunt drag me to church sunday)
i was meaningless
and i wondered if life
would give me a chance to mean

i found a new life in the withdrawal from all things
not like my image

when i was a teen-ager i usta sit
on front steps conversing
the gym teachers son with embryonic eyes
about the essential essence of the universe
(and other bullshit stuff)
recognizing the basic powerlessness of me

but then i went to college where i learned
that just because everything i was was unreal
i could be real and not just real through withdrawal
into emotional crosshairs or colored bourgeoisie intellectual
pretensions
but from involvement with things approaching reality
i could possibly have a life

so catatonic emotions and time wasting sex games
were replaced with functioning commitments to logic and
necessity and the gray area was slowly darkened into
a black thing
for a while progress was being made along with a certain degree
of happiness cause i wrote a book and found a love
and organized a theatre and even gave some lectures on
Black history
and began to believe all good people could get
together and win without bloodshed
then
hammarskjold was killed
and lumumba was killed
and diem was killed
and kennedy was killed
and malcolm was killed
and evers was killed
and schwerner, cheney and goodman were killed
and liuzzo was killed

and stokely fled the country
and le roi was arrested
and rap was arrested
and pollard, thompson and cooper were killed
and king was killed
and kennedy was killed
and i sometimes wonder why i didn't become a debutante
sitting on porches, going to church all the time, wondering
is my eye make-up on straight
or a withdrawn discoursing on the stars and moon
instead of a for real Black person who must now feel
and inflict
pain

1968

Balances

in life
one is always
balancing

like we juggle our mothers
against our fathers

or one teacher
against another
(only to balance our grade average)

3 grains salt
to one ounce truth

our sweet black essence
or the funky honkies down the street

and lately i've begun wondering
if you're trying to tell me something

we used to talk all night
and do things alone together

and i've begun

(as a reaction to a feeling)
to balance
the pleasure of loneliness
against the pain
of loving you

1968

For Theresa

and when i was all alone
facing my adolescence
looking forward
to cleaning house
and reading books
and maybe learning bridge
so that i could fit
into acceptable society
acceptably
you came along
and loved me
for being black and bitchy
hateful and scared
and you came along
and cared that i got
all the things necessary
to adulthood
and even made sure
i wouldn't hate
my mother
or father
and you even understood
that i should love
peppe
but not too much
and give to gary
but not all of me
and keep on moving
til i found me
and now you're sick
and have been hurt
for some time
and i've felt guilty

and impotent
for not being able
to give yourself
to you
as you gave
yourself
to me

1968

STATEMENTS ON POETICS

FRANK MARSHALL DAVIS (from Letter of December 1970)—"Poetry to me represents the writer's way of looking at and interpreting the world. I am primarily a realist who tries to draw vivid pictures with words, hoping the resultant work will have an impact on both black and white Americans."

ROBERT HAYDEN (from Letter of December 1970)—"Every poem I write is for me, in Whitman's phrase, a 'language experiment' and a process of discovery. I value form and rhythm as having an organic relationship to the theme of a poem. I am as much concerned with the sounds and textures of words as I am with their meanings. I write slowly and painstakingly; often work on a poem several years, revising even after publication. Irony together with symbolism modified by realism are, I suppose, characteristic features of my poetry. I think of the writing of poems as one way of coming to grips with inner and outer realities—as a spiritual act, really, a sort of prayer for illumination and perfection. The Baha'i Faith, with its emphasis on the essential oneness of mankind and its vision of world unity, is an increasingly powerful influence on my poetry today—and the only one to which I willingly submit."

DUDLEY RANDALL (from Letter of November 1970)—"My poetics is to try to write poetry as well as I can. I think I have said elsewhere that the function of the poet is to write poetry. My earlier poetry was more formal. Now I am trying to write a looser, more irregular, more colloquial and more idiomatic verse. I abhor logorrhea, and try to make my poems as concentrated and brief as possible."

NAOMI LONG MADGETT (from Letter of November 1970)—"I write in a variety of styles—most often lyric—and on many subjects. Sometimes my poems deal with racial themes (as two in this group do), but more frequently they do not. I feel no duty or compulsion to fight battles or try to change history with my pen. But I know who I am, and if I am sincere in portraying my own personal experiences in blackness, I feel that others who read my work will have shared them and will certainly identify with them."

CONRAD KENT RIVERS (from *Sixes and Sevens,* 1962)—"I write about the Negro because I am a Negro, and I am not at peace with myself or my world.

I cannot divorce my thoughts from the absolute injustice of hate. I cannot reckon with my color. I am obsessed by the ludicrous and psychological behavior of hated men. And I shall continue to write about race, in spite of many warnings—until I discover myself, my future, my real race. I do not wish to capitalize on race, nor do I wish to begin a Crimean War: I am only interested in recording the truth squeezed from my observations and experiences. I am tired of being mis-represented. No white man can dare write my story for me . . . it is for me to do. I write about color because I have no say in the matter. My Muse is blind. I am not ashamed of my flesh. I long to be heard. I am bitter, black, and tired. And I agree with Baldwin: 'Nobody Knows My Name.' 'All the standards for which the western world has lived so long are in the process of break-down and revision; and beauty, and joy, which was in the world before and has been buried so long, has got to come back.' "

LeRoi Jones (from "Black Art," 1965-66)

Poems are bullshit unless they are
teeth or trees or lemons piled
on a step. Or black ladies dying
of men leaving nickel hearts
beating them down. Fuck poems
and they are useful, wd they shoot
come at you, love what you are,
breathe like wrestlers, or shudder
strangely after pissing. We want live
words of the hip world live flesh &
coursing blood. Hearts Brains
Souls splintering fire. We want poems
like fists beating niggers out of Jocks
or dagger poems in the slimy bellies
of the owner-jews. Black poems to
smear on girdlemamma mulatto bitches
whose brains are red jelly stuck
between 'lizabeth taylor's toes. Stinking
Whores! We want "poems that kill."
Assassin poems, Poems that shoot
guns. Poems that wrestle cops into alleys
and take their weapons leaving them dead
with tongues pulled out and sent to Ireland. Knockoff
poems for dope selling wops or slick halfwhite
politicians Airplane poems, rrrrrrrrrrrrrr
rrrrrrrrrrrrrr . . . tuhtuhtuhtuhtuhtuhtuhtuhtuhtuh
. . . rrrrrrrrrrrrrr . . . Setting fire and death to
whities ass. . . .

SONIA SANCHEZ (from Letter of December 1970—"My poems be talkin bout blk/people and the kind of trickology the devil done devised fo us. My poems be love poems for/abt black people. My poems be chants/moans of a blk/woman alone. My poems be talkin bout what can be. And will be if we stop jiven. My poems be."

CLARENCE MAJOR (from Introduction to *The New Black Poetry,* 1969)—"I see our poems, social and political, as scientific new music: these constructs are solar concerts to the infinite tacit incantations of our elegance, as we are, as we long to be. Black radiance.

"This is an elemental art of human communication (or vice versa) sweetly prodding the ornamented deadweight of *what* is left white folks from Greek, Roman equivalents. Our poems function like universal *mandalas* (circles) while they continually liberate our spirits. They are death cries to the pimp *par excellence* of the recent capitalist stages of the world, testimonies against the brutal psychological engravings of his base self-profit oriented psychology, his sham stance.

"These poems speak the immortal language of symbolic and mystic love —the black power hissing is not only the cold blue nature of their pristine compassion but their drama: the firm way they educate . . . .

"Properly, we black poets in our unadorned passage through the sad cycles of life in these Western juxtapositions are aligned with the social and political struggles of visionary peoples who seek ultimately to renew the world, especially to authenticate this society.

"Black poets here are practically and magically involved in collective efforts to trigger real social change, correction throughout the zones of this republic. We are mirrors here, and we know that anybody who has ultimate faith in the system is our enemy. Such people are obstacles. Our weapons are cultural, our poems. Like any concept, any art form, with an impetus in Afro-American nationalism, our poems exist primarily for and go directly to our central human needs, the people, our *shauku* (strong desire). Our minds are the strategy-drawing-boards of a social revolutionary background! Dragons breathing black fire! The experience of our 'eyes,' what the sounds of our spirits unearth . . .!"

JULIA FIELDS (from Letter of December 1970)—"As for my 'poetics,' I do not believe that poetry can have a great influence on the minds of the populace outside the institutions—church, school, home. It seems to me that poetry as 'we "unfortunately" know it' is meant to serve the purpose of academic and racialist or class propaganda. Perhaps it has served its purpose for this era."

DON L. LEE (from Preface of *Don't Cry, Scream,* 1969)—"Black poetry is written for/to/about & around the lives/spiritactions/humanism & total existence of blackpeople. Blackpoetry in form/sound/word usage/intonation/rhythm/repetition/direction/definition & beauty is opposed to that which is now (& yesterday) considered poetry, i.e., whi-te poetry. Blackpoetry in its purest form is diametrically opposed to whi-te poetry. Whereas, blackpoets deal in the concrete rather than the abstract (concrete: art for people's sake; black language or Afro-american language in contrast to standard english, &c.). Blackpoetry moves to define & legitimize blackpeople's reality (**that** which is real to us). Those in power (the unpeople) control and legitimize the negroes' (the realpeople's) reality out of that which they, the unpeople, consider real. That is, to the unpeople the television programs **Julia** and **The Mod Squad** reflect their vision of what they feel the blackman **is** about or **should** be about. So, in effect, blackpoetry is out to negate the negative influences of the mass media; whether it be TV, newspapers, magazines or some white boy standing on a stage saying he's a 'blue eyed soul brother.' "

BIOGRAPHICAL NOTES

ARNA BONTEMPS—Born 1902 in Alexandria, Louisiana; grew up in California and graduated from Pacific Union College and University of Chicago. Served for twenty-two years as librarian at Fisk University. Poetry first appeared in the *Crisis* magazine in 1924. Winner in 1926 and 1927 of the Alexander Pushkin Award for Poetry from *Opportunity*. Also in 1927 his "Nocturne at Bethesda" won first prize in the *Crisis* poetry contest. Author of *Personals* (Breman, 1963). Other books include three novels: *God Sends Sunday* (Harcourt, 1931), *Black Thunder* (Macmillan, 1936) and *Drums at Dusk* (Macmillan, 1939); four anthologies: *Golden Slippers* (Harper, 1941), *The Poetry of the Negro 1746-1970* (Doubleday, 1970) with Langston Hughes, *American Negro Poetry* (Hill & Wang, 1963), *The Book of Negro Folklore* (Dodd, Mead, 1958) with Langston Hughes, and more than twelve children's books, biographies and histories. Currently teaching at Mt. Holyoke College.

GWENDOLYN BROOKS—Born 1917 in Topeka, Kansas; raised in Chicago and graduated from Wilson Junior College. *A Street in Bronzeville* (Harper, 1945) paved the way for an award from the American Academy of Arts and Letters in 1946 and two Guggenheim Fellowships for creative writing, 1946 and 1947. Second volume of poems, *Annie Allen* (Harper, 1949) won the Pulitzer Prize for Poetry in 1950. Other publications include a novel, *Maud Martha* (1953), and four books of poetry: *Bronzeville Boys and Girls* (1956), *The Bean Eaters* (1960), *Selected Poems* (1963) and *In the Mecca* (1968), all with Harper. Named Poet Laureate for the state of Illinois in 1968. Currently teaching at Northeastern Illinois State College, Columbia College and Elmhurst College in Chicago.

STERLING A. BROWN—Born 1901 in Washington, D. C.; graduated from Williams College and Harvard University. Professor of English at Howard University for forty years. Early poems appeared in the late twenties in *Opportunity*. Author of *Southern Road* (Harcourt, Brace, 1932). Awards include a Guggenheim Fellowship for creative writing. Other publications include *Negro Poetry and Drama* (Associates in Negro Folk Education, 1937), *The Negro in American Fiction* (Associates in Negro Folk Education, 1937), and *The Negro Caravan* (Dryden, 1941), a comprehensive anthology edited with Arthur Davis and Ulysses Lee.

LUCILLE CLIFTON—Born 1935 on East Coast; attended Howard University. Mother of six children. Poems have appeared in *Negro Digest* and *The Massachusetts Review.* Author of *Good Times* (Random House, 1969). Currently working on two children's books.

COUNTEE CULLEN—Born 1903 in New York City; graduated from New York University and Harvard University. Early poems won numerous prizes from leading magazines of the twenties, including *Opportunity* and *Crisis.* Author of *Color* (Harper, 1925), *Copper Sun* (Harper, 1927), *Caroling Dusk* (Harper, 1927), *The Ballad of the Brown Girl* (Harper, 1928), *The Black Christ* (Harper, 1929), *One Way to Heaven* (Harper, 1932), *The Medea and Some Poems* (Harper, 1935), and other books. Awards include the Witter Bynner Poetry Prize, a Harmon Gold Award in literature, and a Guggenheim Fellowship. Died in 1946.

MARGARET DANNER—Born 1923 in Pryorsburg, Kentucky; educated at Roosevelt College, Loyola University, and Northwestern University. Poems began appearing during fifties in *Voices* and *Poetry: A Magazine of Verse.* Author of *Impressions of African Art Forms* (Broadside, 1968). Former assistant editor of *Poetry* and founder of Boone House, a center for writers and artists in Detroit. Awards include a John Hay Whitney Fellowship, Harriet Tubman Award, and AMSAC grant. Other publications include *To Flower* (Boone House, 1963) and *Poem Counterpoem* (Broadside, 1966), with Dudley Randall. Currently poet-in-residence at LeMoyne Owens College.

FRANK MARSHALL DAVIS—"Born Arkansas City, Kan., Dec. 31, 1905. Attended Kansas State College, helped start and first editor of *Atlanta Daily World,* 1931, feature editor Associated Negro Press, 1934, executive editor, 1940 to 1948, resident of Hawaii from 1948 to present. Author of *Black Man's Verse* (Black Cat Press, 1935), *I Am the American Negro* (Black Cat Press, 1937), and *47th Street* (Decker Press, 1948). Rosenwald Fellow in Poetry, 1937. Has finished autobiography and new book of poems."

JULIA FIELDS—Born 1938 in Uniontown, Alabama; graduated from Knoxville College in Tennessee and attended Breadloaf Writers Conference in New England. Poems have been published in the *Negro Digest, The Massachusetts Review, Beyond the Blues, American Negro Poetry, New Negro Poets: USA, For Malcolm,* and other little magazines and anthologies. Currently teaching in North Carolina.

NIKKI GIOVANNI—Born 1943 in Knoxville, Tennessee; graduated from Fisk University. Author of *Black Feeling Black Talk* (Afro-Arts, 1968), *Black Judgement* (Afro-Arts, 1968), and *Re: Creation* (Broadside, 1970). Presently working on the autobiography of Nina Simone (with Nina Simone) and teaching at Livingstone College, Rutgers University.

ROBERT HAYDEN—Born 1913 in Detroit, Michigan; graduated from Wayne State University and the University of Michigan. Taught English at Fisk University for twenty-two years. Poems have appeared in *Poetry, Atlantic Monthy, Phylon, Negro Digest,* and other little magazines. Author of *Heart-Shape in the Dust* (Falcon, 1940). Has won Hopwood Award for Poetry in 1942, Grand Prize for Poetry at First World Festival of Negro Arts in 1965, and Russell Loines Award for Poetry in 1970. Other publications include *A Ballad of Remembrance* (Breman, 1962), *Selected Poems* (October House, 1966), *Kaleidoscope* (Harcourt, Brace, 1967), and *Words in the Morning Time* (October House, 1970). Currently a professor of English at the University of Michigan.

LANGSTON HUGHES—Born 1902 Joplin, Missouri; educated at Columbia University and Lincoln University. Early poems won numerous prizes in the popular magazines of the twenties, including *Crisis* and *Opportunity.* Collections of verse include *The Weary Blues* (Knopf, 1926), *Fine Clothes to the Jew* (Knopf, 1927), *The Dream Keeper* (Knopf, 1932), *Shakespeare in Harlem* (Knopf, 1942), *Fields of Wonder* (Knopf, 1947), *One-Way Ticket* (Knopf, 1949), *Montage of a Dream Deferred* (Holt, 1951), *Selected Poems* (Knopf, 1959), *Ask Your Mama* (Knopf, 1961), and *The Panther & the Lash* (Knopf, 1967). Poetry has been translated into every major language and he has won many awards, including a Harmon Award, Guggenheim Fellowship, Rosenwald Fellowship, an American Academy of Arts and Letters grant, and the Spingarn Medal. Books include *The Poetry of the Negro: 1746–1970* with Arna Bontemps, *New Negro Poets: USA* (Indiana, 1964), *The Book of Negro Folklore* with Arna Bontemps, *The Book of Negro Humor,* and numerous other publications. Died in 1967.

TED JOANS—Born in 1928 in Cairo, Illinois; graduated from Indiana University. Began reading his poems in Greenwich Village coffee houses in the fifties and has been a nomadic bard, jazz trumpeteer, and painter ever since. Author of *Black Pow-Wow* (Hill & Wang, 1969). Works in progress include *Spadework: An Autobiography of a Hipster* and *Afrodisia,* a volume of poems.

LEROI JONES—Born 1934 in Newark, New Jersey; graduated Howard University. Early poems appeared in *Big Table, The New American Poetry, Evergreen Review,* and other little magazines. Collections of verse include *Preface to a Twenty Volume Suicide Note* (Totem/Corinth, 1961), *The Dead Lecturer* (Grove, 1963), and *Black Magic Poetry: 1961–1967* (Bobbs-Merrill, 1969). Awards include a John Hay Whitney Fellowship, a Guggenheim Fellowship, and an Obie for *Dutchman,* judged the best off-Broadway play of 1963-64.

Publications include a novel, a collection of short stories, several plays, and other books. Presently spiritual leader of the Community Development and Defense Organization and director of Spirit House, both in Newark.

BOB KAUFMAN—Born c. 1935 in San Francisco, California. Poems first appeared in *Beatitude* in San Francisco in the late fifties. In 1959 and 1960 Lawrence Ferlinghetti published two of his poems as City Lights broadsides. Other publications are *Solitudes Crowded with Loneliness* (New Directions, 1965) and *Golden Sardine* (City Lights, 1967).

KEORAPETSE KGOSITSILE—Born 1938 in Johannesburg, South Africa; has been in exile since 1961; attended colleges on East Coast. Poems and essays have appeared in *Journal of Black Poetry, Soulbook, Negro Digest, Pan African Journal,* and other little magazines. Author of *Spirits Unchained* (Broadside, 1969) and *For Melba* (Third World, 1970).

ETHERIDGE KNIGHT—Born 1933 in Corinth, Mississippi; "died in Korea from a shrapnel wound and narcotics resurrected me. I died in 1960 from a prison sentence and poetry brought me back to life." Poems have appeared in *Negro Digest, Journal of Black Poetry,* and *For Malcolm.* Author of *Poems from Prison* (Broadside, 1968).

DON LEE—Born 1942 in Detroit, Michigan; attended college in Chicago. Poems and essays have appeared in *Negro Digest, Journal of Black Poetry, Freedomways,* and other little magazines. Collections of verse include *Think Black* (1967), *Black Pride* (1968), *Don't Cry, Scream* (1969), and *We Walk the Way of the New World* (1970), all published by Broadside Press. Books scheduled for publication in 1971 are *Selected and New Poems* and *Dynamite Voices: Black Poets of the 1960's.* Currently teaching at Howard University.

AUDRE LORDE—Born 1934 in New York City; graduated Hunter College and Columbia University. Poems have appeared in *Negro Digest, Journal of Black Poetry, Beyond the Blues, New Negro Poets: USA,* and other magazines and anthologies. Author of *The First Cities* (Poets, 1968) and *Cables to Rage* (Breman, 1970).

CLAUDE MCKAY—Born 1891 in Clarendon, Jamaica; came to United States in 1912 and attended Tuskegee Institute and Kansas State University. Was associate editor of *The Liberator* under Max Eastman. Poems appeared in many magazines and anthologies of the twenties, including *The Liberator, Opportunity,* and *Crisis.* Collections of verse include *Songs of Jamaica* (Gardner, 1912), *Spring in New Hampshire* (Richards, 1920), *Harlem Shadows* (Harcourt, Brace, 1922), and *Selected Poems* (Bookman Associates, 1953).

Books of fiction are *Home to Harlem* (Harper, 1928), *Banjo* (Harper, 1929), *Gingertown* (Harper, 1932) and *Banana Bottom* (Harper, 1933). Died in 1948.

NAOMI LONG MADGETT—Born 1923 in Norfolk, Virginia; graduated from Virginia State College and Wayne State University. Poems have appeared in *Negro Digest, Freedomways, Phylon,* and numerous other magazines and anthologies. Author of *Songs to a Phantom Nightingale* (Fortuny's, 1941), *One and the Many* (Exposition, 1956), and *Star by Star* (Harlo, 1965). Currently an associate professor of English at Eastern Michigan University.

CLARENCE MAJOR—Born 1936 in Atlanta, Georgia; grew up and attended school in Chicago. Poems have been published in *Negro Digest, Journal of Black Poetry, Soulbook* and many other little magazines and anthologies. Books include *Swallow Lake* (Wesleyan, 1970), a collection of verse, *The New Black Poetry* (International, 1969), an anthology, and *All-Night Visitors* (Olympia, 1969), a novel. Works in progress include two collections of verse.

GLORIA C. ODEN—Born 1923 in Yonkers, New York; graduated from Howard University. Poems have appeared in *The Saturday Review, The Poetry Digest, American Negro Poetry, Kaleidoscope,* and other magazines and anthologies. Author of *The Naked Frame* (1952), which won her a John Hay Whitney Fellowship. Presently teaching at University of Maryland.

DUDLEY RANDALL—Born 1914 in Washington, D. C.; graduated from Wayne State University and the University of Michigan. Poems have appeared in *Midwest Journal, Negro Digest, Negro History Bulletin, Beyond the Blues, American Negro Poetry, Kaleidoscope,* and other magazines and anthologies. Author of *Poem Counterpoem* (Broadside, 1966) with Margaret Danner, *Cities Burning* (Broadside, 1968), and *Love You* (Breman, 1970). Other books include *For Malcolm* (Broadside, 1967) with Margaret Burroughs and *Black Poetry* (Broadside, 1969), an anthology. Works in progress include an anthology of black poets and another volume of verse. Currently publisher of "the most important black press in America," librarian and poet-in-residence at the University of Detroit.

CONRAD KENT RIVERS—Born 1933 in Atlantic City, New Jersey; graduated from Wilberforce University. Poems have been published in *Negro Digest, Kenyon Review, Antioch Review, Sixes and Sevens, Kaleidoscope, American Negro Poetry,* and other magazines and anthologies. Author of *Perchance to Dream, Othello* (Wilberforce, 1959), *These Black Bodies and This Sunburnt Face* (Free Lance, 1962) and *The Still Voice of Harlem* (Breman, 1968). Died in 1968.

SONIA SANCHEZ—Born 1935 in Birmingham, Alabama; graduated from

Hunter College. Taught in first Black Studies Program at San Francisco State College. Poems have appeared in *Negro Digest, Journal of Black Poetry, Nommo, Soulbook,* and other little magazines and anthologies. Author of *Homecoming* (Broadside, 1969), and *We A BaddDDD People* (Broadside, 1970). Book of poems for children scheduled for publication in 1971. Presently teaching at Livingstone College, Rutgers University.

A. B. SPELLMAN—Born 1935 in Nixonton, North Carolina; graduated from Howard University. Poems have been published in *Yugen, Negro Digest, Beyond the Blues, New Negro Poets: USA, Black Fire* and *The New Black Poetry.* Author of *The Beautiful Days* (Poets, 1964) and *Four Lives in the Bebop Business* (Pantheon, 1967). Currently working on a biography of Billie Holiday.

MELVIN B. TOLSON—Born 1898 in Moberly, Missouri; graduated from Lincoln University and Columbia University. Taught for twenty-two years at Wiley College in Texas. "Dark Symphony" won a prize at Negro American Exposition in Chicago. Commissioned to write a poem for the Liberian Centennial and International Exposition. Author of *Rendezvous with America* (Dodd, Mead, 1944), *Libretto for the Republic of Liberia* (Twayne, 1953) and *Harlem Gallery* (Twayne, 1965). Died in 1966.

JEAN TOOMER—Born 1894 in Washington, D. C.; educated at the University of Wisconsin. Poems appeared in such little magazines of the twenties as *Broom, Little Review, S 4 N,* and *Crisis.* Author of *Cane* (Boni & Liveright, 1923), a book of poetry and poetic sketches. Died in 1967.

MARGARET WALKER—Born 1915 in Birmingham, Alabama; graduated from Northwestern University and Iowa State University. *For My People* (Yale, 1942) won the Yale University Younger Poets competition in 1942. Awards include a Rosenwald Fellowship and a Houghton Mifflin Fellowship for *Jubilee* (Houghton, Mifflin, 1966), a novel. Poems have appeared in many anthologies. Currently teaching at Jackson State College in Mississippi.

SELECTED BIBLIOGRAPHY

I. ANTHOLOGIES

Bontemps, Arna, ed. *American Negro Poetry.* New York: Hill and Wang, 1963.

Brawley, Benjamin G., ed. *Early Negro American Writers.* Chapel Hill: University of North Carolina, 1935.

Breman, Paul, ed. *Sixes and Sevens.* London: Breman, 1962.

Brown, Sterling A., Arthur P. Davis, and Ulysses Lee, eds. *The Negro Caravan.* New York: Dryden, 1941.

Chapman, Abraham, ed. *Black Voices.* New York: Dell, 1968.

Emanuel, James A., and Theodore Gross, eds. *Dark Symphony.* New York: Free Press, 1968.

Hayden, Robert, ed. *Kaleidoscope.* New York: Harcourt, Brace and World, 1967.

Hughes, Langston, and Arna Bontemps, eds. *The Poetry of the Negro 1746–1970.* rev. ed. New York: Doubleday, 1970.

Johnson, Charles S., ed. *Ebony and Topaz.* New York: Opportunity, 1927.

Johnson, James W., ed. *The Book of American Negro Poetry.* rev. ed. New York: Harcourt, Brace, 1931.

Jones, LeRoi, and Larry Neal, eds. *Black Fire.* New York: Morrow, 1968.

Kerlin, Robert T., ed. *Negro Poets and Their Poems.* Washington: Associated, 1923, 1935.

Major, Clarence, ed. *The New Black Poetry.* New York: International, 1969.

Pool, Rosey E., ed. *Beyond the Blues.* Kent: Hand and Flower, 1962.

Robinson, William, Jr., ed. *Early Black American Poets.* Dubuque: William C. Brown, 1969.

Turner, Darwin T., ed. *Black American Literature: Poetry.* Columbus: Charles E. Merrill, 1969.

II. BOOKS, BOOKLETS, AND BROADSIDES

Bontemps, Arna. *Personals.* London: Breman, 1963.

Brooks, Gwendolyn. *A Street in Bronzeville.* New York: Harper, 1945.

__________. *Annie Allen.* New York: Harper, 1949.

__________. *Bronzeville Boys and Girls.* New York: Harper, 1956.

__________. *The Bean Eaters.* New York: Harper, 1960.

__________. *Selected Poems.* New York: Harper and Row, 1963.

__________. *In the Mecca.* New York: Harper and Row, 1968.

________________. *Riot.* Detroit: Broadside, 1969.
________________. *"We Real Cool."* Broadside 6. Detroit: Broadside.
________________. *"The Wall."* Broadside 19. Detroit: Broadside.
Brown, Sterling A. *Southern Road.* New York: Harcourt, Brace, 1932.
Clifton, Lucille. *Good Times.* New York: Random House, 1969.
Cullen, Countee. *Color.* New York: Harper, 1925.
________________. *The Ballad of the Brown Girl; and Old Ballad Retold.* New York: Harper, 1927.
________________. *Copper Sun.* New York: Harper, 1927.
________________. *The Black Christ and Other Poems.* New York: Harper, 1929.
________________. *The Medea and Some Poems.* New York: Harper, 1935.
________________. *On These I Stand.* New York: Harper, 1947.
Danner, Margaret. *To Flower.* Detroit: Boone House, 1963.
________________. *Impressions of African Art Forms.* Detroit: Broadside, 1968.
________________ and Dudley Randall. *Poem Counterpoem.* Detroit: Broadside, 1969.
________________. "Not Light, Nor Bright, Nor Feathery." Broadside #22. Detroit: Broadside.
Davis, Frank Marshall. *Black Man's Verse.* Chicago: Black Cat, 1935.
________________. *I Am the American Negro.* Chicago: Black Cat, 1937.
________________. *47th Street.* Prairie City: Decker, 1948.
Fields, Julia. "I Heard a Young Man Saying." Broadside #10. Detroit: Broadside.
Giovanni, Nikki. *Black Feeling Black Talk.* New York: Afro-Arts, 1968.
________________. *Black Judgement.* New York: Afro-Arts, 1968.
________________. *Re: Creation.* Detroit: Broadside, 1970.
________________. "All I Gotta Do." Broadside #41. Detroit: Broadside.
Hayden, Robert. *Heart-Shape in the Dust.* Detroit: Falcon, 1940.
________________. *A Ballad of Remembrance.* London: Breman, 1962.
________________. *Selected Poems.* New York: October House, 1966.
________________. *Words in the Mourning Time.* New York: October House, 1970.
________________. "Gabriel." Broadside #3. Detroit: Broadside.
Hughes, Langston. *The Weary Blues.* New York: Knopf, 1926.
________________. *Fine Clothes to the Jew.* New York: Knopf, 1927.
________________. *The Dream Keeper and Other Poems.* New York: Knopf, 1932.
________________. *Scottsboro Limited: Four Poems and a Play in Verse.* New York: Golden Stair, 1932.
________________. *Shakespeare in Harlem.* New York: Knopf, 1942.
________________. *Fields of Wonder.* New York: Knopf, 1947.
________________. *One-Way Ticket.* New York: Knopf, 1949.
________________. *Montage of a Dream Deferred.* New York: Knopf, 1951.

____________. *Selected Poems.* New York: Knopf, 1959.
____________. *Ask your Mama: 12 Moods for Jazz.* New York: Knopf, 1961.
____________. *The Panther and the Lash.* New York: Knopf, 1967.
____________. "Backlash Blues." Broadside #13. Detroit: Broadside.
Joans, Ted. *Black Pow-Wow.* New York: Hill and Wang, 1969.
Jones, LeRoi. *Preface to a Twenty-Volume Suicide Note.* New York: Totem/Corinth, 1961.
____________. *The Dead Lecturer.* New York: Grove, 1964.
____________. *Black Magic Poetry: 1961–1967.* New York: Bobbs—Merrill, 1969.
____________. "A Poem for Black Hearts." Broadside #7. Detroit: Broadside.
Kaufman, Bob. "Second April." Broadside. San Francisco: City Lights, 1959.
____________. "Abomunist Manifesto." Broadside. San Francisco: City Lights, 1960.
____________. *Solitudes Crowded with Loneliness.* New York: New Directions, 1965.
____________. *Golden Sardine.* San Francisco: City Lights, 1967.
Kgositsile, Keorapetse. *Spirits Unchained.* Detroit: Broadside, 1969.
____________. *For Melba.* Chicago: Third World, 1970.
Knight, Etheridge. *Poems from Prison.* Detroit: Broadside, 1968.
____________. "2 Poems for Black Relocation Centers." Broadside #21. Detroit: Broadside.
Lee, Don. *Think Black.* Detroit: Broadside, 1967.
____________. *Black Pride.* Detroit: Broadside, 1968.
____________. *Don't Cry, Scream.* Detroit: Broadside, 1969.
____________. *We Walk the Way of the New World.* Detroit: Broadside, 1970.
____________. "Back Again, Home." Broadside #16. Detroit: Broadside.
____________. "Assassination." Broadside #25. Detroit: Broadside.
____________. "One Sided Shoot-Out." Broadside #33. Detroit: Broadside.
Lorde, Audre. *The First Cities.* New York: Poets, 1968.
____________. *Cables to Rage.* London: Breman, 1970.
McKay, Claude. *Songs of Jamaica.* Kingston: Gardner, 1912.
____________. *Spring in New Hampshire.* London: Richards, 1920.
____________. *Harlem Shadows.* New York: Harcourt, Brace, 1922.
____________. *Selected Poems.* New York: Bookman, 1953.
Madgett, Naomi Long. *Songs to a Phantom Nightingale.* New York: Fortuny's, 1941.
____________. *One and the Many.* New York: Exposition, 1956.
____________. *Star by Star.* Detroit: Harlo, 1965.
____________. "Sunny." Broadside #11. Detroit: Broadside.

Major, Clarence. *Swallow Lake.* Middletown: Wesleyan, 1970.
Oden, Gloria C. *The Naked Frame.* 1952.
Randall, Dudley, and Margaret Danner. *Poem Counterpoem.* Detroit: Broadside, 1966.
__________. *Cities Burning.* Detroit: Broadside, 1968.
__________. *Love You.* London: Breman, 1970.
__________. "Ballad of Birmingham." Broadside #1. Detroit: Broadside.
__________. "Dressed All in Pink." Broadside #2. Detroit: Broadside.
__________. "Booker T. and W. E. B." Broadside #8. Detroit: Broadside.
Rivers, Conrad Kent. *Perchance to Dream, Othello.* Wilberforce: Wilberforce, 1959.
__________. *These Black Bodies and This Sunburnt Face.* Cleveland: Free Lance, 1962.
__________. *The Still Voice of Harlem.* London: Breman, 1968.
Sanchez, Sonia. *Homecoming.* Detroit: Broadside, 1969.
__________. *We A BaddDDD People.* Detroit: Broadside, 1970.
__________. "Liberation Poem." Broadside #34. Detroit: Broadside.
Spellman, A. B. *The Beautiful Days.* New York: Poets, 1964.
Tolson, Melvin B. *Rendezvous with America.* New York: Dodd, Mead, 1944.
__________. *Libretto for the Republic of Liberia.* New York: Twayne, 1953.
__________. *Harlem Gallery.* New York: Twayne, 1965.
__________. "The Sea Turtle and the Shark." Broadside #5. Detroit: Broadside.
Toomer, Jean. *Cane.* New York: Boni and Liveright, 1923.
__________. "Song of the Son." Broadside #15. Detroit: Broadside.
Walker, Margaret. *For My People.* New Haven: Yale University, 1942.
__________. *Prophets for a New Day.* Detroit: Broadside, 1970.
__________. "Ballad of the Free." Broadside #4. Detroit: Broadside.

III. RECORDS AND TAPES

Bontemps, Arna. *Anthology of Negro Poets.* Folkways FL 9791.
__________. *An Anthology of Negro Poets in the USA.* Folkways FP 9792.
__________. *Negro Poetry for Young People.* Folkways FC 7114.
Brown, Sterling, and Langston Hughes. *Sterling Brown and Langston Hughes Read Their Poems.* Folkways FP 9790.
Giovanni, Nikki. *Re: Creation.* Broadside Tape.
Hughes, Langston. *The Dream Keeper.* Folkways F 7104.

Kgositsile, Keorapetse. *Spirits Unchained.* Broadside Tape.
Knight, Etheridge. *Poems from Prison.* Broadside Tape.
Lee, Don. *Don't Cry, Scream.* Broadside Tape.
____________. *We Walk the Way of the New World.* Broadside Tape.
Randall, Dudley. *Cities Burning.* Broadside Tape.
Sanchez, Sonia. *Homecoming.* Broadside Tape.
____________. *We A BaddDDD People.* Broadside Tape.

IV. CHIEF LITTLE MAGAZINES

Beatitude (1959–1961) San Francisco, California
Big Table, ed. Paul Carroll, Chicago, Illinois
Black Dialogue, ed. Edward Spriggs, New York, N. Y.
Black Expression, ed. Eugene Perkins, Chicago, Illinois
Black World (formerly *Negro Digest*), ed. Hoyt Fuller, Chicago, Illinois
The Crisis, ed. Henry L. Moon, New York, N. Y.
Evergreen Review, ed. Barney Rosset, New York, N. Y.
Journal of Black Poetry, ed. Joe Gonclaves, San Francisco, California
Nommo, Chicago, Illinois
Opportunity: Journal of Negro Life (1923–1949), New York, N. Y.
Poetry, eds. Karl Shapiro and Henry Rago, Chicago, Illinois
Soul Book, ed. Bobb Hamilton, Berkeley, California
Yugen, ed. LeRoi Jones, New York, N. Y.

V. ADDRESSES OF BLACK PRESSES

Black Dialogue Press, P. O. Box 1019, Harlem, N. Y. 10027
Broadside Press, 15205 Livernois, Detroit, Michigan 48238
The Crisis Publishing Co., Inc., 1790 Broadway, New York, N. Y. 10019
Free Black Press, 7512 S. Cottage Grove, Chicago, Illinois 60619
Jihad Productions, P. O. Box 663, Newark, N. J.
Johnson Publishing Co., Inc. *(Black World)* 1820 S. Michigan Ave., Chicago, Illinois 60616
Journal of Black Poetry Press, 922 Haight St., San Francisco, California 94117
Third World Press, 7850 S. Ellis Ave., Chicago, Illinois 60619

INDEX OF AUTHORS

INDEX OF FIRST LINES